NATO

What You Need To Know

NATO

What You Need To Know

MEDEA BENJAMIN and DAVID SWANSON

Preface by Jeffrey D. Sachs

OR Books
New York · London

First printing 2024

Cataloging-in-Publication data is available from the Library of Congress.
A catalog record for this book is available from the British Library.

paperback ISBN 978-1-68219-520-8 • ebook ISBN 978-1-68219-521-5

CONTENTS

What You Need to Know About NATO

Jeffrey D. Sachs

This is an indispensable primer. It can save your life—indeed all of our lives. NATO is a clear and present danger to world peace, a war machine run amok, that operates beyond the democratic control of the citizenry of the NATO countries.

The war machine lines the pockets of the arms contractors at the core of NATO, U.S. companies like Lockheed Martin and Northrop Grumman, and Europe's arms manufacturers, including Britain's BAE Systems, Germany's Rheinmetall, and Sweden's BAE Systems Bofors. In doing so, NATO also sucks one nation after another into the vortex of war, instability, displacement, and poverty. During the past 30 years, NATO has fomented a vast arc of violence stretching from Libya to Afghanistan and with many victims in between.

NATO also draws us ever closer to nuclear Armageddon. The war in Ukraine was caused by the United States's long-standing obsession to expand NATO to Ukraine and Georgia, with the goal of surrounding Russia in the Black Sea. The Ukraine war has brought the world's two largest nuclear superpowers, Russia and the U.S., into a direct and escalating military confrontation.

We urgently need the clarity of this volume since NATO operates through propaganda and misdirection. NATO, we are told by our governments, is peace-loving, even as it provokes one war after another. NATO, we are told by our governments, is defensive, even as it violently topples other governments. NATO, we are told by the alliance's own founding treaty, is about the North Atlantic even as it spreads its warmongering to Africa and Asia.

The supreme irony about NATO is that its great expansion has taken place after the end of the Cold War. The original purpose of NATO, after all, was to defend Western Europe against a possible invasion by the Soviet Union. When the Soviet Union ended in 1991, NATO should have ended with it. Instead, NATO expanded, from 16 members in 1991 to 32 members today. NATO's eastern push was designed to weaken Russia if not topple it or break it apart.

As this volume carefully documents, there was no shortage of warnings by leading diplomats that NATO enlargement would inflame tensions with Russia and thereby endanger the peace. The dean of U.S. diplomacy, George Kennan, warned in 1997 "that expanding NATO would be the most fateful error of American policy in the entire post-cold-war era." Fifty leading foreign policy experts wrote to President Clinton in 1997 with the same message.

We are reminded in detail in these pages of NATO's utterly dismal track record of the past 30 years. Its military forays have led to years, and sometimes decades, of destabilization in the targeted countries, including Bosnia, Serbia, Afghanistan, Libya, and Ukraine among others. In Orwellian fashion, all of this violence and instability has been justified as defending "the rules-based order," even as NATO has repeatedly violated the core precepts of the UN Charter.

The sad truth is that NATO is neither a defensive alliance nor a bulwark of global rules. After 1992 it became an expeditionary force to promote a delusional U.S. hegemony. The very aim of U.S. hegemony is an act of supreme hubris, as if 4% of the world's population could truly presume to dictate to the other 96%. The United States's presumption of primacy, and its use of NATO to achieve it, not only runs against both common sense and international law, but also against the limits of the United States's wisdom and power.

As the reader will learn in the pages that follow, there are real life-saving alternatives to the endless wars. We can and must build a safer world based on the UN Charter, peace, and diplomacy. As the authors compellingly advise, it is the time for a global grassroots movement to Say No to NATO and No to War.

Jeffrey D. Sachs is a professor at Columbia University and President of the UN Sustainable Development Solutions Network.

Introduction

We wrote this book on the occasion of the 75th anniversary of NATO's founding in 1949. Prior to the Russian invasion of Ukraine, NATO looked like a tired, stale organization filled with bickering members in search of a reason to stay together. A generation after the collapse of communism, the Western alliance was adrift and confused. There was little reason to fear Russia, a country whose GDP was equivalent to Spain and which spent five times less on its military than the 28 EU states combined. And the mighty U.S. military, the most powerful, high-tech force on Earth, was licking its wounds from its failures in Afghanistan and Iraq.

French President Emmanuel Macron called NATO "brain dead."[1] Donald Trump called it obsolete.[2] Allies wondered if NATO under Donald Trump would really intervene if they were attacked. One European analyst compared U.S. forces in Europe to the Berlin wall before its fall. "Strong and powerful from the outside, it can collapse from one day to the other."[3]

But when Russian troops poured across the Ukrainian border on February 24, 2022, NATO got a new lease on life. Divisions in the ranks were quickly papered over and the United States, which had lost so much credibility with its disastrous "war on terror," was once again leading the charge to "save the free world."

But while NATO has been temporarily resurrected, the unity will surely be short-lived. For beneath the surface, NATO is still a Cold War relic that should have dissolved when the Soviet Union fell apart.

In this book, we go through NATO's origins, including its purpose as stated in its charter and the *real* purposes—not only checking Soviet expansion but defeating communist and socialist movements throughout Europe, crushing overseas liberation movements, and making sure the U.S. was the dominant power in Europe.

We explain why NATO, rather than declaring victory and folding when the Soviet Union fell apart, not only forged ahead but expanded right up to Russia's borders.

We also detail NATO's history of aggression—its military forays into Bosnia, Kosovo, Afghanistan, Iraq, and Libya. Bringing its history of aggression up to date, we look at NATO's role in the Ukraine conflict, including its provocative call for Ukraine to become a NATO member, its role in the 2014 coup, its training and arming Ukrainian forces in preparation for war with Russia, and its quashing of negotiations that could have ended the war in its first month.

Our chapter on NATO "partners" shows NATO as a global behemoth with partners that encircle the globe from Colombia to Mongolia to Australia. We look at how decisions are made (spoiler alert: the U.S. calls the shots) and the truth behind U.S. complaints that NATO members are not paying their "fair share."

The chapters on international law and nuclear weapons reveal how NATO has repeatedly violated the precepts of the UN Charter and how the placement of U.S. nuclear weapons in five European nations violates the 1970 Treaty on the Non-Proliferation of Nuclear Weapons and the Treaty on the Prohibition of Nuclear Weapons.

We point out the divisions in the alliance over the years—from France wanting military autonomy to Turkey opposing Sweden's membership to the very different perspectives on Israel's war on Gaza.

Looking ahead, we expose NATO's dangerous plans with regards to Russia and China, and we wrap up with the most important discussion—what are the alternatives to NATO and how can we build a movement to clip NATO's wings.

In commemorating the alliance's 75th anniversary, U.S. Senator James Risch of the Foreign Relations Committee commended NATO for its role in maintaining security and defending freedom, calling it "the most successful political-military alliance in the history of the world."[4]

Professor Jeffrey Sachs says just the opposite. He calls NATO "a clear and present danger to world peace, a war machine run amok."

Who is right? Read on and make your own decision.

1

When And Why Was NATO Formed?

On April 4, 1949, as the contours of a new Cold War were emerging after the devastation of the Second World War, foreign ministers from 12 countries came together in Washington, D.C., to sign the North Atlantic Treaty and form the North Atlantic Treaty Organization (NATO). The original members were Belgium, Canada, Denmark, France, Iceland, Italy, Luxembourg, the Netherlands, Norway, Portugal, the United Kingdom, and the United States.

According to NATO, the alliance was created with a three-pronged aim: deterring Soviet expansionism, forbidding the revival of nationalist militarism in Europe through a strong North American presence on the continent, and encouraging European political integration. Or, as the alliance's first Secretary General Lord Ismay quipped, its purpose was "to keep the Soviets out, the Americans in, and the Germans down."[1]

The Treaty,[2] also known as the Washington Treaty, is a mere 1,100 words, with 14 short articles and a brief introduction, which states:

"The Parties to this Treaty reaffirm their faith in the purposes and principles of the Charter of the United Nations and their desire to live in peace with all peoples and all governments. They are determined to safeguard the freedom, common heritage and civilisation of their peoples, founded on the principles of democracy, individual liberty and the rule of law. They seek to promote stability and well-being in the North Atlantic area. They are resolved to unite their efforts for collective defense and for the preservation of peace and security. They therefore agree to this North Atlantic Treaty."

NATO was initially designed as a 20-year commitment. Article 13 of the North Atlantic Treaty states: *"After the Treaty has been in force for twenty years, any Party may cease to be a Party one year after its notice of denunciation has been given to the Government of the United States of America, which will inform the Governments of the other Parties of the deposit of each notice of denunciation."* So far, while there have been major divisions within the Alliance and threats of pulling out (France withdrew from the NATO Military Command Structure in 1966 but rejoined in 2009), no nations have withdrawn.

The first articles echo the UN Charter by committing the members to settle international disputes by peaceful means and to refrain from the threat or use of force. As you will see, these most basic principles are the very ones that NATO completely abandoned after the end of the Cold War, as it acted as a junior partner in the United States' global military ambitions and illegal wars.

In other articles of the Treaty, members commit to consult together whenever the territorial integrity, political independence, or security of any of them is threatened, and to eliminate conflict in economic policies and encourage economic collaboration.

The treaty then goes on to talk about developing the capacity to resist armed attacks and support each other when a member's territorial integrity, political independence, or security is threatened.

So, after acknowledging their binding commitments to the UN Charter, including to the peaceful resolution of disputes and the renunciation of the threat or use of force, the Treaty comes to the heart of the matter, which is that this is a military alliance, not a group of friendly nations joining hands to reiterate the commitments to peace that they already made when they signed the UN Charter.

The most controversial and weighty article is Article 5. Its first paragraph states the following: "*The Parties agree that an armed attack against one or more of them*

7

in Europe or North America shall be considered an attack against them all and consequently they agree that, if such an armed attack occurs, each of them, in exercise of the right of individual or collective self-defense recognized by Article 51 of the Charter of the United Nations, will assist the Party or Parties so attacked by taking forthwith, individually and in concert with the other Parties, such action as it deems necessary, including the use of armed force, to restore and maintain the security of the North Atlantic area."[3]

Article 5 obligates members to assist other members by military means, but it permits each nation to decide for itself what action it should take to respond to an armed attack on a NATO ally. A member may decide that, instead of responding with force, it will just send military equipment or impose economic sanctions on the aggressor, or it could conceivably organize nonviolent action or appeal to the International Court of Justice. But Article 5 is widely interpreted as an obligation to assist by military means.

Even if a NATO ally is attacked and Article 5 is invoked, member countries still have to abide by their own laws. Article 11 of the Treaty explains that "its provisions [shall be] carried out by the Parties in accordance with their respective constitutional processes."

Under the United States Constitution and war powers laws, that would require securing express authorization from Congress before sending the military into a conflict zone or otherwise using force, since Congress has the sole constitutional power to declare war and is responsible for military appropriations and oversight. In practice, however, successive presidents have used force in violation of the Constitution and the UN Charter, and Congress has consistently failed to exercise its authority to prevent them from doing so.

Article 5 has been invoked only once in NATO's history, in response to the terrorist crimes of September 11, 2001, in the United States. But it was wrongly invoked in that case to support the U.S. invasion of Afghanistan, which had not attacked the U.S. or any other NATO member. As former Nuremberg prosecutor Ben Ferencz told NPR at the time, "It is never a legitimate response to punish people who are not responsible for the wrong done." (See the section on NATO in Afghanistan.)

Was NATO truly formed to "safeguard the shared values of democracy"?

NATO was presented in its founding treaty as a means to safeguard the members' shared values of democracy, individual liberty, and the rule of law. But despite the democratic language of the Treaty, the real glue that brought NATO countries together was opposition to communism and socialism. This meant not just trying to counter the strength of the USSR and the military structures it had built across Eastern Europe, but also opposing communist movements within Western Europe and opposing revolutionary, anticolonial struggles around the globe.

With respect to the Soviet Union, NATO's founders would say that they were simply responding to Soviet expansionism and the Cold War that was already under way. But the creation of NATO, and the exclusion of the Soviets, actually intensified and institutionalized the Cold War. The Soviet counterpart, the Warsaw Pact, was only created six years later, as a response to NATO.

One of NATO's real purposes was to stifle the growth of communism within war-torn Western Europe itself. In many Western European countries, communists and socialists had led the resistance to German and Italian occupation during WWII. So after the war, leftist parties were quite popular and naturally expected to play important roles in government. They won elections to national parliaments, regional and city councils, and were allied with powerful unions, especially in Italy and France.

The United States began funding, arming, and training reactionary forces that would wage a long and hidden war against Europe's thriving socialist and communist movements. These initiatives were institutionalized under NATO, which became a bulwark against communism throughout Europe and beyond.[4] Instead of promoting the "shared values of democracy," NATO actually helped destroy popular movements and narrow democratic choices.

The first additions to NATO, Greece and Turkey in 1952, rendered meaningless NATO's founding principle of promoting "stability and well-being in the North Atlantic area" since Turkey is nearly 2,000 miles from the North Atlantic and Greece is not much closer. But also because neither was a democracy.

Greece was accepted after its ruthless Western-backed government had killed or jailed the last of the partisans who had liberated it from the Nazis. Greece remained a NATO member, even under a brutal military junta from 1967 to 1974.

Turkey's membership gave NATO military control of the Bosporus Strait—the only navigational waterway between the Mediterranean Sea and the Black Sea and a choke point for the Soviet ports of Odessa and Sevastopol. Its membership extended NATO's encirclement of the Soviet Union and guaranteed that Turkey would not become a Soviet ally.

Within a decade of joining the alliance, the elected governments of both Turkey and Greece were toppled in coups d'état. Turkey experienced military coups in 1960, 1971, and 1980. But that did not affect their NATO membership.

In both cases, their strategic value to the alliance clearly outweighed any concerns with the "principles of democracy" mentioned in the North Atlantic Treaty.

How did NATO relate to anti-colonial struggles?

Among the 12 founding members, one-third—Britain, France, Belgium, and Portugal—still directly possessed vast empires in Africa and were waging vicious campaigns to try to hold onto their colonies. In the case of France, the original version of the treaty even specified that NATO obligations applied to any attack on "the Algerian Departments of France,"[5] effectively acknowledging Algeria as an integral part of France. NATO supported France during the Algerian War for independence from 1954 to 1962, one of the longest and bloodiest wars of decolonization.

Portugal was still ruled by the dictator Antonio Salazar when it became a founding member of NATO, and was admitted mainly because the U.S. military wanted a base in the Azores—islands that are strategically located in the North Atlantic. NATO and NATO member countries armed and equipped the Portuguese regime, enabling it to wage a 25-year colonial war in its African colonies of Guinea-Bissau, Angola, and Mozambique.

The freedom struggles in Africa were repeatedly discussed in NATO council meetings throughout the 1950s and 1960s, and their suppression was a component of its general counter-revolutionary political, diplomatic, and military strategy.

At an Asian-African Conference in Bandung in 1955, Indian Prime Minister Jawaharlal Nehru called NATO "the most powerful protector of colonialism," and said that Morocco, Algeria, and Tunisia "would probably have been independent if it were not for NATO."[6]

In 1965, Guinean revolutionary Amílcar Cabral described how weapons from NATO countries—including the U.S., Germany, France, and Italy—were used against liberation forces throughout Africa.[7]

What has been the U.S. interest in NATO?

From the U.S. perspective, any war between the United States and the Soviet Union was going to put Europeans on the front lines, both as combatants and as mass-casualty victims. So one purpose of NATO was to make sure that the people of Europe played their assigned roles in U.S. war plans.

NATO provided a vehicle for imposing U.S. leadership over Western nations. It tied Europe to U.S. military, geopolitical, and economic interests. It made Europeans dependent on U.S. military power to protect them from the USSR. It also prevented France, Germany, and their partners in what became the European Union from developing Europe into a truly independent counterweight to the power of the United States in the Western world.

A State Department analysis in the mid-1960s concluded that NATO "remains essential to the U.S. as a well-established and easily available instrument for exercising American political influence in Europe."[8]

NATO also had an economic purpose. In its founding "Strategic Concept" paper, NATO conceived the integration of its members to be "not just military, but also political, economic, and psychological.[9] NATO countries were expected to disseminate an anti-communist worldview and to promote pro-capitalist, free trade economies.

Privatizing the economy has been a key requisite for entering NATO. In a meeting in Poland in 1997, then Senator Joe Biden, addressing Poland's interest in joining NATO, said that all NATO member states have free-market economies with the private sector playing the leading role, and he asserted that Poland's large, state-owned enterprises should be placed into the hands of private owners. "For Poland to be in the vanguard of Western economies in the 21st century," he insisted, "businesses like banks, the energy sector, the state airline, the state copper producer, and the telecommunications monopoly will have to be privatized."[10]

NATO has helped to fortify U.S. global economic interests. From privatization to dollar hegemony to international trade, including thwarting bilateral trade agreements between NATO members and the Soviet Union, U.S. administrations have used U.S. military dominance as leverage to guarantee European cooperation on economic issues of vital interest to Washington.

While U.S. political leaders have complained over the years about NATO members not carrying their weight financially, U.S. military leaders have noted NATO's economic benefits. When the U.S. got involved in 1994 in Kosovo, Deputy Assistant Secretary of Defense David Ochmanek wrote in a memorandum that the U.S. had to intervene in "messy security problems in Europe" if we "want a seat at the table when the Europeans make decisions about trade and financial policy."

General William Odom, who was National Security Agency Director from 1985 to 1988, maintained that "only a strong NATO with the U.S. centrally involved can prevent Western Europe from drifting into national parochialism and eventual regression from its present level of economic and political cooperation."[11]

This rationale has continued over the years. A 1992 leaked Pentagon document about post-Cold War military planning argued that U.S. military might was essential for stability in Europe, and that the United States must therefore "discourage the advanced industrialized nations from challenging our leadership or even aspiring to a larger global or regional role."[12]

It went on to argue that U.S. Cold War alliances, including NATO, ensure "a prosperous, largely democratic, market-oriented zone of peace and prosperity that encompasses more than two-thirds of the world's economy." This makes maintaining these alliances the United States's "most vital" foreign policy priority.

Another U.S. economic interest has been the U.S. weapons industry. In his book *The Spoils of War*, Andrew Cockburn documents a major role in NATO expansion played by U.S. weapons companies hoping to sell their products in the former Warsaw Pact. A lobby group called the U.S. Committee to Expand NATO was run by a vice president of Lockheed Martin. And nations like Romania, despite a desperate domestic crisis in funding human needs, were made to understand that only by making huge purchases of U.S. weapons could they become NATO members.

What was the Warsaw Pact?

After World War II, when Russia was invaded from the West for the third time since 1800 and 27 million of its people perished, the USSR made sure to end that war with a buffer zone of friendly communist governments between it and Germany.

Winston Churchill publicly coined the term "Iron Curtain" in 1946 to describe the post-World War II division of Europe into enemy camps, and the formation of NATO. Then the Warsaw Pact made his image a reality, with a solid line of militarized borders stretching from north to south across Europe.

The Warsaw Pact[13] was formed as a counterpoint to NATO in 1955, five days after NATO admitted West Germany as a new member, and nine days after the official end of the U.S., British, and French military occupation of West Germany.

In reality, Britain did not leave its last base in Germany until 2020, France still has one today, and the U.S. still stations at least 48,000 troops at 45 bases across Germany in 2024. You could call this a win-win situation for U.S. militarism, giving it a new front-line ally and arms-industry customer in West Germany, and later in a united Germany, but never really ending its own military occupation.

The original members of the Warsaw Pact were the Soviet Union, East Germany, Poland, Hungary, Romania, Bulgaria, Czechoslovakia, and Albania. (Albania withdrew in 1968 in protest of the Soviet invasion of Czechoslovakia.)

A little-known fact is that one year before forming the Warsaw Pact, the USSR, fearing the revival of German militarism in West Germany, asked if it, too, could join NATO. This proposition, which could have radically changed the course of history by folding the USSR into the European security blanket, was rejected by the U.S., the UK, and France. The Soviet desire to be part of a European collective security was clear in the opening paragraph of the Warsaw Pact, which stated "their desire for the establishment of a system of European collective security based on the participation of all European states irrespective of their social and political systems."

The Pact then declared that a remilitarized West Germany and the integration of West Germany into the North Atlantic bloc increased the danger of another war and constituted a threat to the national security of European states.[14]

As a member of the Warsaw Pact, East Germany was allowed to re-arm, creating the National People's Army to counter the rearmament of West Germany. Europe settled into an uneasy, fearful stand-off, symbolized by the construction of the Berlin Wall in 1961, and overshadowed by the danger of annihilation by the U.S. and Soviet nuclear arsenals.

Just as the United States has always been the dominant partner in NATO, so the Soviet Union dominated the Warsaw Pact. It also used force to prevent the rise of more independent governments in Hungary in 1956, when the government of Imre Nagy tried to leave the Warsaw Pact, and Czechoslovakia in 1968.

Despite U.S. Cold War rhetoric condemning the Soviet uses of force in Hungary and Czechoslovakia, both President Eisenhower in 1956 and President Johnson in 1968 resisted calls to intervene militarily. Recognizing the danger of another world war, the U.S. decided to accept the Soviet use of force in its "sphere of influence" in Eastern Europe.

During the 1960s and 1970s, the two camps battled each other via global proxy wars, and brought the world to the brink of a nuclear conflict in the 1962 Cuban Missile Crisis. But they avoided open war with each other, despite amassing nuclear arsenals that threatened the very existence of humanity.

By the late 1980s, anti-Soviet and anti-communist movements throughout Eastern Europe were so widespread that the Pact started falling apart. In 1988, Mikhail Gorbachev, then leader of the Soviet Union, abandoned the Brezhnev Doctrine, which proclaimed that any threat to socialist rule in any of the Soviet Bloc states was a threat to all of them and therefore justified intervention.

This allowed Eastern and Central European countries to change their political and economic systems, leading to sweeping changes in the region. By the late 1980s, Gorbachev spoke of a "common European home." There was hope that the Cold War and the bipolar alliance system it had engendered would come to an end.

In 1990, East Germany left the Warsaw Pact to prepare for reunification with West Germany. Czechoslovakia, Hungary, Poland, and Bulgaria all announced they, too, would withdraw from the Pact. The Warsaw Pact was officially dissolved on July 1, 1991, just prior to the dissolution of the Soviet Union itself at the end of that year.

Many observers expected that the demise of the Warsaw Pact would mean the demise of NATO, since the collapse of the Soviet Union and the Warsaw Pact had made it redundant. But they were wrong. Rather than accepting the new reality by declaring victory and dismantling its war machine, NATO did the opposite. It embraced this power dividend and rejected the peace dividend that its members' people expected and deserved.

2

NATO Expansion

Instead of disbanding, NATO has grown from its original 12 members to 32 members in 10 rounds of enlargement. NATO says it has an "open door" policy, meaning that any European country can solicit membership. According to Article 10 of the Alliance's founding document, NATO membership is open to any "European state in a position to further the principles of this Treaty and to contribute to the security of the North Atlantic area."[1]

What are the criteria for joining?

While there is no membership checklist for interested nations, candidates for membership are, in theory, supposed to meet the following criteria: "functioning democratic political system based on a market economy; fair treatment of minority populations; a commitment to resolve conflicts peacefully; an ability and willingness to make a military contribution to NATO operations; and a commitment to democratic civil-military relations and institutions."[2] Their military forces are supposed to be under civilian control, and they are supposed to have a commitment to work toward interoperability with NATO forces.

The steps to join NATO are as follows:

Step 1: Accession talks with NATO in Brussels. This involves discussions to determine if an invitee meets the requirements of NATO membership. As of 1999, a Membership Action Plan was put in place to help applicants make the necessary political, economic, defense, resource, security, and legal reforms.

Step 2: Letter of intent sent to NATO secretary general in which the invitee confirms its acceptance of NATO commitments and presents a timetable of reforms.

Step 3: Accession protocols signed by NATO members.

Step 4: Accession protocols ratified by NATO member governments according to their national procedures. In the U.S., this requires a two-thirds majority of the Senate.

Step 5: Secretary general invites the potential member to accede to the treaty.

Step 6: Invitee accedes to the treaty according to its national procedures.

Step 7: After depositing its instruments of accession with the U.S. Department of State, an invitee becomes a NATO member.

The membership process is a long one, usually taking many years. This is especially true if a member has to make economic and legal changes.

Decisions to add new members must be made by unanimous agreement of all current members, which has been a sticking point over the years when members have had disagreements. For many years, Greece blocked NATO membership for Macedonia, and only assented when the country officially changed its name to North Macedonia in 2018. More recently, Hungary held up Sweden's entry for 18 months, finally relenting in February 2024.

Over the years, the ratification process has also stirred debates inside the U.S. Senate. Opposition to NATO expansion has come from both conservative Republicans and liberal Democrats, with concerns ranging from increased costs, over-extension of U.S. military commitments overseas, and the consequences of poisoning relations with Russia by adding former Soviet nations. But in all cases, the expansionists have eventually prevailed.

When and where did NATO expand?

In 1955 West Germany was incorporated, furthering the rift with the Soviet Union. It took almost three decades, however, for further growth, with a newly democratic Spain joining in 1982 after the fall of the fascist Franco regime.

In 1990, East and West Germany were united, and the reunified Germany was incorporated in NATO. It was following the breakup of the Soviet Union, however, that several former Soviet bloc countries wanted to join the alliance out of fear of Russian aggression. Russian military actions, including the First Chechen War, were among the factors driving Central and Eastern European countries to push for NATO membership.

From the U.S. perspective, NATO expansion was seen as a way to take advantage of Russian weakness and ensure that no independent European security arrangement would emerge to challenge U.S. hegemony.

Amid much criticism from Russia and internal debate in NATO countries, Poland, Hungary, and the Czech Republic joined in 1999. While the people of Poland and Hungary supported the move, there was significant opposition in the Czech Republic. Polls showed support for NATO membership at 50-60%,[3] while only a minority believed the country faced any external threat, and disagreed on what it might be.

This expansion took place despite promises to the Russians that NATO would not move toward Russia's border. Those promises were not codified in a formal treaty but, according to declassified U.S., Soviet, German, British, and French documents posted in the National Security Archive at George Washington University, Western leaders gave multiple assurances to Soviet President Mikhail Gorbachev and other Soviet officials throughout the process of German unification in 1990 and 1991.[4]

U.S. Secretary of State James Baker's famous "not one inch eastward" assurance in his meeting with Gorbachev on February 9, 1990, was only one of these many promises, but they were all broken in the ensuing years.

A 1990 State Department memorandum advised that it was not in the best interest of NATO or the United States to grant NATO membership to Eastern European states. It warned that, if the U.S. organized an anti-Soviet coalition on its border, "such a coalition would be perceived very negatively by the Soviets."[5]

Debate within the U.S. government as to whether enlargement of NATO was feasible or desirable began during the George H. W. Bush administration. By mid-1992, a view emerged within that administration, and later in the Clinton administration, that NATO enlargement could be a positive move that would strengthen and expand Euro-U.S. hegemony.

In 1997, 50 prominent foreign policy experts warned President Clinton not to expand NATO eastward, calling it a policy error of "historic proportions" that would "unsettle European stability."[6] They also said it would be expensive and unnecessary, given that Russia posed no threat to its Western neighbors. Clinton ignored the advice, as he was reportedly more worried about the impact that saying "no" to Poland would have on Polish-American voters in the Midwest. The Clinton administration ended up making aggressive NATO enlargement part of its foreign policy.

Clinton's own hawkish Secretary of State, Madeleine Albright, wrote in her memoir that Boris Yeltsin and the Russian public "were strongly opposed to enlargement, seeing it as a strategy for exploiting their vulnerability and moving Europe's dividing line to the east, leaving them isolated."[7] But in 1998, when NATO incorporated the three former Warsaw Pact countries, NATO was indeed right against Russia's borders.

In a *New York Times* article in 1997, George Kennan, the intellectual father of U.S. containment policy during the Cold War, warned "that expanding NATO would be the most fateful error of American policy in the entire post-cold-war era." Russia, he said, would be "little impressed with American assurances that it reflects no hostile intentions."[8]

The following year, he warned[9] in a *New York Times* interview that NATO expansion was the beginning of a new Cold War: "I think the Russians will gradually react quite adversely and it will affect their policies. I think it is a tragic mistake. There was no reason for this whatsoever. No one was threatening anybody else."

Some of the most prescient warnings came from President Joe Biden's eventual CIA director, William J. Burns, who held various key positions in the State Department over the years. Back in 1995, when he was a political officer at the U.S. Embassy in Moscow, Burns reported that "hostility to early NATO expansion is almost universally felt across the domestic political spectrum here."[10]

Responding to the Clinton administration's move to bring Poland, Hungary, and the Czech Republic into NATO, Burns called that decision premature at best and needlessly provocative at worst. "As Russians stewed in their grievance and sense of disadvantage, a gathering storm of 'stab in the back' theories slowly swirled, leaving a mark on Russia's relations with the West that would linger for decades," he wrote.

NATO's big expansion came in 2004. Seven countries joined—Bulgaria, Estonia, Latvia, Lithuania, Romania, Slovakia, and Slovenia. Russia was particularly upset by the addition of the three Baltic states—Estonia, Latvia, and Lithuania—because they were countries that had been part of the Soviet Union and had hosted Russian military bases until 1995. They had even been part of the Russian Empire during the Czarist era.

That was followed by the accession of Albania and Croatia in 2009, Montenegro in 2017 and North Macedonia in 2020.

Looking back on NATO's provocative policy toward Russia over the past quarter century, it is clear why U.S. government officials sent dire warnings that continuing to expand the most heavily armed military alliance in history closer and closer to Russia's borders would end in confrontation.

Vladimir Putin himself expressed his views very clearly in a foreign policy address at the Munich Conference on Security Policy in March 2007, when he complained that "NATO has put its frontline forces on our borders" and that NATO enlargement "represents a serious provocation that reduces the level of mutual trust. And we have the right to ask: Against whom is this expansion intended? And what happened to the assurances our Western partners made after the dissolution of the Warsaw Pact?"[11]

Proponents of NATO enlargement tend to frame the issue of adding new members or partners as a choice that individual countries should be able to make. If a country wants to be part of NATO, why shouldn't it have that right? We can see why countries would want to join. As long as NATO exists as an exclusive military alliance led by the United States and other major military powers, the hypothetical protection it offers smaller states is almost too good to be true, while the obligations of new members are quite flexible.

But this only compounds the threat that NATO poses to any country that it excludes and views as an enemy, such as Russia, as it gradually encircles it with powerful weapons and armed forces. Whether intended or not, every country in Eastern Europe that joins NATO increases the threat felt by Russia, taking all of Europe and the entire world a step closer to the danger of a civilization-ending nuclear war.

Why did Finland and Sweden join NATO?

NATO's triumphalism may have reached its apex with the accession of Finland in 2023 and Sweden in 2024. The catalyst for these nations to join the alliance was the 2022 Russian invasion of Ukraine.

Swedish Prime Minister Magdalena Andersson said, "Russia's full-scale aggression against a sovereign and democratic neighbor was a watershed moment for Sweden and my government has come to the conclusion that the security of the Swedish people will be best protected within the NATO alliance."[12]

Sweden's decision to join NATO marks a sharp turn from a tradition of neutrality and military non-alignment that stretches back to the Napoleonic period. But despite its official neutrality, Sweden had participated in NATO missions in Bosnia, Kosovo, and Afghanistan. Eight Swedish-built Gripen fighter jets and two support planes took part in the savage bombing and covert invasion of Libya in 2011.

Sweden has, over the years, developed a strong weapons industry and has been a major exporter. Saab, the Swedish manufacturer of Gripen fighter jets, was ranked as having the 39th largest arms revenue in the world in 2022.[13] Company CEO Micael Johansson said publicly that joining NATO's "inner circle" would give the nation's arms industry access to greater markets. "We have already started to see potential contracts coming in," he said, "and we continue to work on other common acquisitions from the NATO perspective."[14]

Before Russia's invasion of Ukraine, public opinion was against Sweden joining NATO. The first poll to register majority support for NATO membership (51%) came in March 2022, just after the Russian invasion.

Sweden's membership was delayed by 20 months due to opposition from Hungary and Turkey. Hungary caved when offered more Swedish weapons, and Turkey gave in when Sweden agreed to take a tougher stand against the PKK (the Kurdistan Workers Party), which Turkey has been fighting for decades.

Like Sweden, Finland also has an advanced arms industry that stands to profit from integration into NATO's lucrative arms market, the facility to purchase more of the latest U.S. and allied weaponry for its own military, and the ability to collaborate on joint weapons projects with firms in larger NATO countries.

But Finland's entry into NATO is particularly tragic, since it is giving up a respected tradition as a global peacemaker. Under President Urho Kekkonen, Finland led two years of negotiations that led to the 1975 Helsinki Accords, an important step in Cold War détente, in which 35 countries from both sides of the Iron Curtain agreed on 10 principles they would all follow in their relations with each other.

In 2008, former Finnish President Martti Ahtisaari was awarded the Nobel Peace Prize for his lifelong peacemaking work in Namibia, Northern Ireland, Kosovo, and around the world. Certainly joining NATO is a betrayal of Finland's upstanding tradition of peacemaking.

While public support for joining NATO in Finland has historically rested at 20-30%, that quickly jumped to 60% after Russia invaded Ukraine, illustrating how Europe's security dilemma can lead even a strongly neutral country into its spiral of escalation.

But Finland's leaders have always been more pro-NATO than its people. As a NATO partner since 1997, they sent Finnish troops to take part in the U.S. and NATO occupation of Afghanistan, where two Finnish troops were killed.

A study by the Finnish Institute for International Affairs found that Finnish troops "repeatedly engaged in combat as part of the military operation that was now led by NATO, and had become a party in the conflict." Finland's proclaimed objective was "to stabilize and support Afghanistan to enhance international peace and security," but, in practice, this was outweighed by "its desire to maintain and strengthen its foreign and security policy relations with the U.S. and other international partners, as well as its effort to deepen its collaboration with NATO."[15]

As Finland confronts Russia across its 830-mile border, the longest border between Russia and any NATO country, Finland will be just as impotent as it was in Afghanistan to affect the momentum of the NATO war machine's rising conflict with Russia.

Finland will find that its tragic choice will leave it, like Ukraine, dangerously exposed on the front lines of a war directed from Moscow, Washington, and Brussels that it can neither win, nor independently resolve, nor prevent from potentially escalating into World War III.

3

NATO'S History of Aggression

NATO has always presented itself to the world as a defensive alliance. However, lacking a peer competitor after the end of the Cold War and the dissolution of the Warsaw Pact, NATO was no more able than the United States itself to resist the temptation to use military force offensively and aggressively, in violation of the UN Charter. This led to NATO involvement in U.S.-led military adventures, leaving chaos and misery in its wake, in Serbia, Afghanistan, Iraq, and Libya.

Coupled with NATO's expansion across Europe and its position as the most heavily armed military alliance in history, its readiness to act as a junior partner in U.S. aggression poses an implicit threat of devastating military violence to any countries involved in international disputes with the United States or other NATO members.

Article 2 (3) of the UN Charter states, "All Members shall settle their international disputes by peaceful means in such a manner that international peace and security, and justice, are not endangered."[1]

When a powerful military alliance like NATO violates the solemn commitments of its members to the UN Charter, despite reiterating them in NATO's own founding document, how can any country locked in a security dilemma with NATO members take the risk of relying on assurances that its purpose is entirely defensive, when this has already proven to be false many times over?

And yet, instead of even trying to address the obvious international security concerns raised by its expansion and illegal war-making, NATO remains lost in an echo chamber of misplaced triumphalism and dishonest, one-sided threat assessments that render it incapable of learning from its own history.

What was NATO's role in Bosnia-Herzegovina?

In 1992, as Yugoslavia began to disintegrate under pressure from Western-backed nationalist movements, NATO deployed ships and planes to enforce UN sanctions against the government of Yugoslavia.

As the wars in Yugoslavia escalated in 1994, NATO launched the first ever combat operation in its 45-year history to enforce a UN-authorized "no-fly zone" over Bosnia. U.S. warplanes shot down four Bosnian Serb warplanes, and NATO eventually conducted hundreds of airstrikes in 1994 and 1995. Then, under the Dayton peace accords, NATO deployed up to 60,000 armed troops in Bosnia from 1995 until 2004.

These military interventions into Bosnia's civil conflict crossed the fateful red line that defined NATO as a purely defensive alliance. In Bosnia, NATO used military force against an insurgent movement that had not attacked, or even threatened, a NATO member. Military intervention in Bosnia was unpopular among the public in many NATO countries and it countered French and British efforts to broker a negotiated settlement.

For decades afterwards, Bosnia remained a dysfunctional ward of NATO and the West, while NATO eagerly embraced its new role as a junior partner in the United States's increasingly aggressive uses of military force against other countries and forces.

Why did NATO get involved in Serbia and Kosovo?

The dismemberment of Yugoslavia continued, leaving only Serbia and Montenegro as a rump "Federal Republic of Yugoslavia" by 1999. Then President Clinton and NATO leaders ordered an illegal bombing campaign that dropped 23,000 bombs on Serbia, followed by the NATO invasion and occupation of the Serbian province of Kosovo.[2]

U.S. and NATO leaders presented the war to the
Western public as a "humanitarian intervention" to protect Kosovo's majority ethnic Albanian population from
ethnic cleansing at the hands of Yugoslav president
Slobodan Milosevic. But that narrative has been unrave-
ling piece by piece ever since, and 10 leaders of NATO's
principal Kosovar ally in the war, the CIA-backed Kosovo
Liberation Army (KLA), now sit in prison cells at The
Hague, on trial for gruesome crimes carried out under
cover of the NATO bombing campaign.

These prisoners include the KLA's leader, Hashim
Thaçi, who rose after the war to become prime minister
and then president of Kosovo. The crimes against humanity he is charged with include a scheme in which the KLA
sent people detained during the war across the border to
Albania, where they murdered them and removed their
internal organs to sell on the international organ trans-
plant market.

These allegations were first investigated by Carla Del
Ponte, the chief prosecutor of the International Criminal
Tribunal for the former Yugoslavia from 1999 to 2007,
but non-cooperation by NATO occupation forces and UN
authorities prevented her from fully investigating them
before her mandate expired.[3]

After Del Ponte wrote about them in a memoir of
her time in Yugoslavia, Dick Marty, an investigator for
the Council of Europe, completed the investigation that

led to the charges at a special court in The Hague.[4] Jack Smith was the lead prosecutor in the trial, until the U.S. Justice Department recalled him to Washington to serve as a special counsel overseeing two of its cases against former president Donald Trump.

From 1996 on, the CIA and Germany's BND intelligence agency had covertly worked with the KLA to instigate and fuel violence and chaos in Kosovo. The CIA spurned mainstream Kosovar nationalist leaders in favor of gangsters and heroin smugglers like Thaçi and his cronies, recruiting them as terrorists and death squads to assassinate Yugoslav police and anyone who opposed them, ethnic Serbs and Albanians alike. As it has done in country after country since the 1950s, the CIA unleashed a civil war that Western politicians and media dutifully blamed on Yugoslav authorities.

By early 1998, even U.S. envoy Robert Gelbard called the KLA a "terrorist group" and the UN Security Council condemned "acts of terrorism" by the KLA and "all external support for terrorist activity in Kosovo, including finance, arms, and training." Once the war was over and Kosovo was occupied by U.S. and NATO forces, CIA sources openly touted the agency's role in manufacturing the civil war that set the stage for NATO intervention.[5]

In September 1998, the UN Security Council passed Resolution 1199, calling for a cease-fire, an international

monitoring mission, the return of refugees, and a political resolution. A new U.S. envoy, Richard Holbrooke,
convinced Yugoslav President Milosevic to agree to a unilateral cease-fire and a 2,000-member verification mission from the Organization for Security and Cooperation
in Europe (OSCE).

Holbrooke persuaded the chair of the OSCE, Polish
Foreign Minister Bronislaw Geremek, to appoint William
Walker, the former U.S. Ambassador to El Salvador during its civil war, to lead the Kosovo Verification Mission.[6]
The U.S. quickly hired 150 Dyncorp mercenaries to form
the nucleus of Walker's 1,380-member team, who used
GPS equipment to map Yugoslav military and civilian
infrastructure for the NATO bombing campaign the U.S.
was already planning.

Walker's deputy, Gabriel Keller, France's former
Ambassador to Yugoslavia, accused Walker of sabotag-
ing the Kosovo Verification Mission, and CIA sources
later admitted that the Mission was a CIA front to coordinate with the KLA and spy on Yugoslavia.

The climactic incident that set the political stage
for the NATO bombing and invasion was a firefight at
a village called Raçak, which the KLA had fortified as a
base from which to ambush police patrols and dispatch
death squads to kill local "collaborators." In January 1999,
Yugoslav police attacked the KLA base in Raçak, leaving
43 men, a woman, and a teenage boy dead.

After the firefight, Yugoslav police withdrew from the village, and the KLA reoccupied it and staged the scene to make the firefight look like a massacre of civilians. When William Walker and a Mission team visited Raçak the next day, they accepted the KLA's massacre story and broadcast it to the world, and it became a critical part of the pretext for the bombing of Yugoslavia and NATO occupation of Kosovo.

Autopsies by an international team of medical examiners found traces of gunpowder on the hands of nearly all the bodies, showing that they had fired weapons.[7] They were nearly all killed by multiple gunshots as in a firefight, not by precise shots as in a summary execution, and only one victim was shot at close range. But the full autopsy results[8] were only published much later, and the Finnish chief medical examiner accused Walker of pressuring her to alter them.

Two experienced French journalists and an AP camera crew at the scene challenged the KLA and Walker's version of what happened in Raçak. Christophe Chatelot's article in *Le Monde* was headlined, "Were the dead in Racak really massacred in cold blood?"[9] and veteran Yugoslavia correspondent Renaud Girard concluded his story in *Le Figaro* with another critical question, "Did the KLA seek to transform a military defeat into a political victory?"[10]

NATO immediately threatened to bomb Yugoslavia, and France agreed to host high-level talks. But instead of inviting Kosovo's mainstream nationalist leaders to the talks in Rambouillet, Secretary Albright flew in a delegation led by KLA commander Hashim Thaçi, until then known to Yugoslav authorities only as a gangster and a terrorist.

Albright presented both sides with a draft agreement in two parts, civilian and military. The civilian part granted Kosovo unprecedented autonomy from Yugoslavia, and the Yugoslav delegation accepted that. But the military agreement would have forced Yugoslavia to accept a NATO military occupation, not just of Kosovo but with no geographical limits, in effect placing all of Yugoslavia under NATO occupation.[11]

When Milosevic refused Albright's terms for what amounted to unconditional surrender, the U.S. and NATO claimed he had rejected peace, and war was the last resort. They did not return to the UN Security Council to try to legitimize their plan, knowing full well that Russia, China, and other countries would reject it. When UK Foreign Secretary Robin Cook told Albright that the British government was "having trouble with our lawyers" over NATO's plan to attack Yugoslavia without authorization from the UN Security Council, she told him to "get new lawyers."[12]

In March 1999, the Kosovo Verification Mission teams were withdrawn and the bombing began. Pascal Neuffer, a Swiss mission observer reported, "The situation on the ground on the eve of the bombing did not justify a military intervention. We could certainly have continued our work. And the explanations given in the press, saying the mission was compromised by Serb threats, did not correspond to what I saw. Let's say rather that we were evacuated because NATO had decided to bomb."[13]

NATO destroyed its list of military targets in Serbia in the first three days, but continued bombing civilian infrastructure in Serbia and Montenegro for 78 days, probably killing thousands of civilians,[14] as it bombed hospitals, schools, bridges, passenger trains, and buses, residential neighborhoods, power stations, the national TV broadcaster, the Chinese Embassy in Belgrade,[15] and other diplomatic sites.[16]

While the United States conducted most of the airstrikes, NATO was a full partner in the operation. Spanish pilots conducted the first airstrikes on the Serbian capital, Belgrade, and British and Norwegian special operations forces were the first NATO troops to land in Pristina, the capital of Kosovo.

The bombing ended when Russia persuaded its Serbian allies to withdraw from Kosovo and agree to a joint NATO-Russian occupying force, as in Bosnia. But before British and Norwegian forces could reach Pristina, Russian forces from Bosnia occupied the only airport.[17]

General Wesley Clark, the U.S. Supreme Allied Commander in Europe, ordered a British officer to "overpower" and "destroy" the Russian forces. The officer refused, and the British commander of NATO forces in Kosovo, General Mike Jackson, backed him up and told Clark, "I'm not going to start the Third World War for you." Jackson told his government he would resign rather than enforce Clark's order. Thankfully, the stand-off was resolved peacefully. Russian forces remained in Kosovo, not under NATO command.

After the NATO invasion, the U.S. military set up the 955-acre Camp Bondsteel in southeastern Kosovo, one of its largest bases in Europe, on its newest occupied territory. Europe's Human Rights Commissioner, Álvaro Gil-Robles, visited Camp Bondsteel in 2002, and exposed it as a secret CIA black site for illegal, unaccountable detention and torture, calling it "a smaller version of Guantanamo."[18]

For the people of Kosovo, the ordeal was not over when the bombing stopped. Far more people had fled the bombing than the so-called "ethnic cleansing" that the CIA provoked to create the pretext for bombing. Former NATO Secretary General Lord Carrington condemned the NATO bombing for causing ethnic cleansing instead of preventing it.[19] A reported 900,000 refugees, nearly half the population, returned to a shattered province now ruled by gangsters and foreign overlords.

Serbs and other minorities became second-class citizens, clinging precariously to homes and communities where many of their families had lived for generations. More than 200,000 Serbs, Roma, and other minorities fled. Camp Bondsteel became the province's largest employer, and U.S. military contractors also sent Kosovars to work in occupied Afghanistan and Iraq.

In 2007, a German military intelligence report described Kosovo as a "Mafia society," based on the "capture of the state" by criminals.[20] The report named Hashim Thaçi, then the leader of the Democratic Party, as an example of "the closest ties between leading political decision makers and the dominant criminal class." In 2000, 80% of the heroin trade in Europe was controlled by Kosovar gangs,[21] and the presence of thousands of U.S. and NATO troops fueled an explosion of prostitution and sex trafficking, also controlled by Kosovo's new criminal ruling class.[22] By 2021, Kosovo's per-capita GDP was only $4,401, the lowest in Europe besides Moldova and Ukraine.[23]

As the web of lies spun by Clinton and Albright has unraveled, and the truth behind their lies has spilled out piece by bloody piece, the war on Yugoslavia has emerged as a case study in how U.S. and NATO leaders mislead us into war. In many ways, Kosovo established the template that U.S. leaders have used to plunge our country and the world into endless war ever since. What U.S. leaders took away from their "success" in Kosovo was that legality, humanity, and truth are no match for CIA-manufactured chaos and lies, and they doubled down on that strategy to plunge the U.S. and the world into endless war, with a subservient NATO along for the ride.

What was NATO's role in Afghanistan?

After the terrorist crimes in the United States on September 11, 2001, NATO invoked Article 5 for the first time in its history and played a major role in the catastrophic 20-year military occupation of Afghanistan.

The United States carried out the initial bombardment and invasion in October 2001, but the UN-backed International Security Assistance Force (ISAF) was set up to train new Afghan military forces just two months later, using forces mainly from NATO countries. In 2003, NATO formally took command of ISAF, and by 2011, it was in command of 132,000 occupation forces from 48 countries, including 90,000 U.S. troops. Even after NATO's ISAF operation ended in 2014, NATO remained in Afghanistan until 2021, in command of 13,000 to 17,000 troops from 36 countries, with half of that force provided by the United States.

The disastrous 20-year Afghan war killed hundreds of thousands of Afghan forces on both sides and hundreds of thousands more civilians, as U.S. and NATO forces dropped 85,000[24] bombs and missiles on the country and conducted tens of thousands of "kill or capture" night raids, most of which targeted innocent civilians.[25] In addition to 2,465 Americans and 455 British troops killed in Afghanistan, nearly 600 troops from other NATO countries were also killed there.[26]

The invasion also displaced millions from their homes, and destroyed more of the country's already war-damaged infrastructure. This bloody quagmire ended in August 2021 with the humiliating rout of Western forces and the return of the very same Taliban government that the United States had attacked, invaded, and occupied the country to remove from power 20 years earlier.

After its chaotic withdrawal, the Biden administration retargeted sanctions on Kabul and seized $9 billion in vital central bank reserves, leaving the economy in ruins and the Afghan people hungry.

In 2012, an Afghan taxi driver in Vancouver told journalist Nicolas Davies, "We defeated the Persian Empire in the 18th century; we defeated the British Empire in the 19th century; we defeated the Soviet Union in the 20th century; now, with NATO, we are fighting 28 countries, but we will defeat them too."

What did this taxi driver know that the leaders of the NATO countries failed to understand? Very possibly, it was exactly what scholar Richard Barnet wrote in a fitting epitaph to the U.S. War on Vietnam in his book *Roots of War* in 1972: "At the very moment the number one nation has perfected the science of killing, it has become an impractical instrument of political domination."

Such is the hubris of Western leaders that even the total defeat of U.S. and NATO forces in Afghanistan barely dented their erroneous assumptions about the power of their forces and weapons to impose their political will on people and countries around the world. Instead of learning from this experience, the U.S and NATO have insanely redirected their defeated war machine against much better-armed enemies like Russia and China.

Did NATO get involved in the illegal U.S. invasion of Iraq?

U.S. plans to invade Iraq in 2003 bitterly divided NATO members, with the result that most NATO members were spared immediate involvement in another catastrophic war. France and Germany were firmly opposed, and joined Russia to oppose the war in the UN Security Council. Two weeks before the invasion, France, Germany, and Russia issued a joint statement that closed the door on any new resolution to authorize the use of force against Iraq. They declared,

"Our common objective remains the full and effective disarmament of Iraq, in compliance with Resolution 1441. We consider that this objective can be achieved by the peaceful means of the inspections.... In these circumstances, we will not let a proposed resolution pass that would authorize the use of force. Russia and France, as permanent members of the Security Council, will assume all their responsibilities on this point."[27]

On March 19, 2003, nonetheless, the United States and Britain invaded Iraq, in flagrant violation of the UN Charter. They unleashed a war that destroyed Iraq, and from which it has never recovered. The only other NATO troops that took an active part in the invasion were small numbers of Danish and Polish special operations forces.

The total number of Iraqis killed quickly became a major front in the U.S. propaganda war to minimize its reputational damage from this self-perpetuating catastrophe. The true number of dead in Iraq is probably in the millions. The country was plunged into decades of chaos from which it has never recovered. Many Iraqis look back with nostalgia on the days of dictator Saddam Hussein.

The hostile military occupation of Iraq spun out of control early on and provoked widespread and effective popular resistance. In August 2003, the UN, hoping to restore some kind of legitimate government in Iraq after the illegal U.S. invasion, established the UN Assistance Mission for Iraq (UNAMI).

Five days later, the Resistance responded to the UN's complicity in the U.S. occupation with a suicide truck bombing that killed 23 people, including the UN Special Representative in Iraq, Sérgio Vieira de Mello, and precipitated the evacuation of 600 UN staff from Iraq.

Several NATO members sent forces to take over "security" from U.S. and British invasion forces in parts of Iraq.[28] Eighteen Italian troops and national police who had replaced U.S. Marines occupying Nasiriyah in southern Iraq were killed when a suicide bomber crashed a tanker truck full of fuel into the gates of the Italian headquarters.

The dead lay in state at the Vittoriano in Rome for several days, as people came from all over Italy to pay their respects, a stark contrast to the secrecy in which the bodies of thousands of U.S. troops were quietly shipped home in the dead of night, and photos of their U.S.-flag-draped coffins were prohibited until 2009.[29]

In 2004, the United States tried to put an Iraqi face on its brutal occupation by appointing an "interim," unelected, Iraqi government. The Iraqi face the U.S. occupation government chose for this role was that of Iyad Allawi, a British MI6 asset since 1978, who was also the figurehead of one of the most spectacular failures in CIA history: its failed coup in Iraq in 1996.[30]

The imposition of Allawi as "interim prime minister" in 2004 provided a transparent cover for the U.S. Marine massacre in Fallujah and the launch of a savage, years-long guerrilla war against the Iraqi Resistance. The U.S. brought in veterans of U.S. wars in Latin America, like Iran-Contra figure Colonel James Steele and the DEA's Steven Casteel, to recruit, train, and unleash Iraqi death squads against the Resistance and the public who supported it.

By the peak of the war in 2006, as many as 1,800 bodies were brought to the morgue in Baghdad each month, while others disappeared without a trace.[31] Western corporate media attributed the deaths to "sectarian violence," ignoring the well-documented role of the occupation government's U.S.-trained death squads as the main perpetrators.

The appointment of the interim government also lured NATO into an active role in the occupation. The first 60 NATO trainers from Canada, Hungary, Italy, the Netherlands, and Norway arrived in Iraq in August 2004 to train senior Iraqi military officers. In December 2004, the mission was expanded to 300 trainers from 16 countries. The program trained 1,250 Iraqi officers in 2005 and, by 2007, 300 Iraqi officers had also been trained outside Iraq in nine NATO countries.

The line between the U.S. occupation and NATO's training mission was blurred by giving U.S. generals joint command of U.S. and NATO training programs in Iraq, and at least six NATO countries still refused to send troops to Iraq (Belgium, France, Germany, Greece, Luxembourg, and Spain), but they agreed to contribute to the training program in other ways.[32]

Other countries with troops in Iraq were already pulling them out. Spain's new Socialist government withdrew its troops in 2004. Bulgaria, Hungary, and Portugal pulled out by the end of 2005, followed by Italy and Norway in 2006, and Lithuania, Poland, and Romania in 2007. The British completed their withdrawal from Basra in 2007.

Several NATO allies also took part in the bombing campaign that dropped over 120,000 bombs and missiles on Iraq and Syria between 2014 and 2021.[33] They destroyed Mosul in Iraq, Raqqa in Syria, and many smaller cities, towns, and villages in Iraq and Syria, in the name of fighting ISIS or Da'esh, the extreme Islamist group spawned by the United States and its Al Qaeda-linked allies in Syria,[34] and by the U.S. war on Iraq.

In 2018, NATO began a new training mission in Iraq, taking over from U.S. forces whose presence was no longer welcome. Six years later, Iraq is still negotiating the removal of those U.S. forces.

In addition to 4,586 U.S. and 182 British troops killed, 106 troops from other NATO countries have also been killed in Iraq.[35]

What was NATO's role in overthrowing Muammar Gaddafi in Libya?

Muammar Gaddafi was a favorite villain of the West and an ally of the USSR, Cuba, Nelson Mandela's African

National Congress, and the Polisario Front in Western Sahara. Gaddafi created a unique form of direct democracy,[36] and he used Libya's oil wealth to provide free healthcare and education, giving Libya the 5th highest GDP per capita in Africa and the highest human development rating in Africa, using the UN index that measures income, health, and education.[37]

Gaddafi also used Libya's wealth to fund projects to give African countries more control of their own natural resources, like a Libyan-funded factory in Liberia to manufacture and export tire-grade rubber instead of raw rubber.[38] He also co-founded the African Union in 2002, which he envisioned growing into a military alliance and a common market with a single currency.

The Libyan Islamic Fighting Group (LIFG), formed by Libyans who had fought with CIA- and Saudi-backed forces in Afghanistan, was paid by the UK's MI6 intelligence agency and Osama bin Laden to try to kill Gaddafi in 1996. The UK gave asylum to some of the group's members, most of whom settled among the large Libyan community in Manchester.

In 2005, the UK did an about-face. It banned LIFG and confiscated its members' passports due to its links with Al-Qaeda. But that all changed again in 2011, when their passports were returned, and MI6 helped many of them travel back to Libya to join the "NATO rebels."[39] One LIFG member, Ramadan Abedi, took his 16-year-old son

Salman with him to Libya. Six years later, Salman struck his own blow for his family's extremist ideology, carrying out a suicide bombing that killed 23 young music fans at an Ariana Grande concert in Manchester in May 2017.

Western leaders' eagerness to overthrow Gaddafi led NATO to attack Libya in March 2011, exploiting UN Security Council Resolution 1973, which only authorized the use of force to protect civilians in Libya.[40] Instead, they waged a bombing campaign and covert war to overthrow the government, rejecting an African Union initiative to resolve the crisis peacefully.[41]

The UN resolution called for an "immediate ceasefire" and prohibited an invasion of Libya, but it authorized a "no-fly zone," which became the pretext for bombing Libya's military and civilian infrastructure with 7,700 bombs and missiles.[42]

Also in violation of the resolution, NATO secretly deployed CIA officers and British, French, Canadian, and Qatari special operations forces to organize and lead Libyan rebel forces on the ground. Altogether, 14 NATO countries took part in the war, along with Sweden, Jordan, Qatar, and the UAE.

A U.S.- and French-led coalition of nine NATO countries and Qatar launched the bombing campaign on March 19, but NATO took full command of all aspects of the war on March 31. Warships from 12 NATO countries enforced a naval blockade against Libya, while eight NATO countries, Qatar, and the UAE conducted airstrikes.

After taking the capital, Tripoli, NATO and its allies cut off food, water, and electricity to the people of Sirte and Bani Walid as they bombarded them for weeks. The combination of aerial, naval, and artillery bombardment, starvation and rebel atrocities on these civilian populations made a final, savage mockery of the UN Security Council's mandate to protect civilians.[43]

Gaddafi was captured in Sirte by NATO-backed rebels, who sodomized him with a knife and summarily executed him, a crime that was gleefully celebrated by Hillary Clinton and other U.S. officials.

In 2016, a parliamentary foreign affairs committee in the UK concluded that a "limited intervention to protect civilians drifted into an opportunistic policy of regime change by military means," resulting in "political and economic collapse, inter-militia and inter-tribal warfare, humanitarian and migrant crises, widespread human rights violations, the spread of Gaddafi regime weapons across the region, and the growth of Isil [Islamic State] in north Africa."[44]

The chaos and civil war unleashed by NATO and its allies raged on for nine years, with competing governments ruling different parts of the country and local militias controlling many smaller areas, until a UN-brokered nationwide cease-fire in 2020.

Human rights groups reported that thousands of black Libyans and sub-Saharan Africans suffered arbitrary detention and appalling abuse at the hands of the militias that the U.S. and its allies helped to take over the country, and that Africans were being bought and sold in slave markets in Libya.[45]

As Libya struggles to dig its way out of this endless chaos, the U.S. and NATO have more or less washed their hands of the crisis they created. In 2023, U.S. foreign aid to Libya was only $45.5 million, a tiny fraction of the estimated $3 billion NATO countries spent to destroy Libya in 2011.[46]

4

NATO in Ukraine, But No Ukraine in NATO?

Since the illegal and tragic Russian invasion of Ukraine, NATO has been intimately involved in supporting Ukraine's efforts to defeat Russia. What is less known is the long history of NATO involvement in Ukraine, how insisting on future NATO membership incensed the Russians, and how NATO members have stymied attempts to find a negotiated solution.

Since the break-up of the Soviet Union, the West has been determined to move Ukraine out of Russia's orbit and integrate it into the West. Ukraine was initially tied to NATO under the Partnership for Peace, which was established in 1994. From 1995 to 2003, NATO conducted annual training exercises with the Ukrainian military at its Yavoriv base near the Polish border, involving up to 1,600 troops from 27 countries.[1] NATO's joint exercises also included naval drills in the Black Sea, despite protests from Moscow and the people of Crimea.

Ukraine's close military relationship with U.S. and NATO forces led it to deploy 1,660 troops to Iraq from 2003 until 2006 under the U.S. military occupation, which led to the deaths of 18 Ukrainian troops.[2] In 2008, President George W. Bush proclaimed that Ukraine was "the only non-NATO country supporting every NATO mission."

Did NATO promise membership to Ukraine?

Plans to incorporate Ukraine into NATO date back to 2002, when Ukraine's President Leonid Kuchma signed an action plan committing Ukraine to join the alliance. His successor, Viktor Yushchenko, was invited to the Brussels NATO Summit in 2005, but the issue did not come to a head until the 2008 NATO Summit in Bucharest.

At that 2008 meeting, U.S. President George W. Bush wanted to offer Ukraine and Georgia a concrete and immediate road map to membership, but that was rejected by other NATO members, particularly Germany and France. U.S. intelligence agencies also warned against it, knowing very well how it would be received by the Russians.

William Burns was by then U.S. ambassador to Moscow and recalled in his book, *The Back Channel*, a missive that he sent to Secretary of State Condoleezza Rice:

"Ukrainian entry into NATO is the brightest of all redlines for the Russian elite (not just Putin). In more than two and a half years of conversations with key Russian players, from knuckle-draggers in the dark recesses of the Kremlin to Putin's sharpest liberal critics, I have yet to find anyone who views Ukraine in NATO as anything other than a direct challenge to Russian interests."[3]

Burns also sent an official 12-point cable to Secretary Rice and Defense Secretary William Gates on February 1, 2008, which was published by WikiLeaks in 2010. It was headed, in all caps: "NYET MEANS NYET [No means No]: RUSSIA'S NATO ENLARGEMENT REDLINES."[4]

Burns wrote: "Not only does Russia perceive encirclement, and efforts to undermine Russia's influence in the region, but it also fears unpredictable and uncontrolled consequences which would seriously affect Russian security interests."

"Experts tell us," Burns continued, "that Russia is particularly worried that the strong divisions in Ukraine over NATO membership, with much of the ethnic-Russian community against membership, could lead to a major split, involving violence or at worst, civil war. Russia would have to decide whether to intervene—a decision Russia does not want to have to face."

The last-minute compromise—which Burns described as the worst of both worlds—was a promise that Ukraine would become a member at some unspecified time in the future.

The issue of NATO membership was divisive inside Ukraine as well. Between 2003 and 2009, Ukrainian public support for NATO membership was never more than 30%[5] and reflected divisions between the pro-Western part of the country in the west and the pro-Russian eastern part.

In the meantime, NATO has continued to deepen its partnership with Ukraine and to push for membership. At NATO's 2023 Summit in Vilnius, the NATO-Ukraine Council was established. NATO declared: "We are helping to transition Ukraine from Soviet-era to NATO equipment and standards. We have also removed the requirement for a Membership Action Plan, significantly shortening Ukraine's path to membership. All Allies agree that Ukraine will become a member of NATO."[6]

What role has NATO played in the conflict with Russia?

Viktor Yanukovych was elected president of Ukraine in 2010. He wanted to follow a policy of neutrality, not to pursue NATO membership, and to maintain good relations with Russia while he negotiated with the European

Union over a possible path to EU membership. This led to an uprising that was supported by the West. It culminated in the violent overthrow of Yanukovych in 2014, and a new pro-Western, anti-Russian government. The pro-Russian regions of Donetsk and Luhansk declared independence and Russia, determined to maintain access to its key base and warm-water port on the Black Sea, took over Crimea. The Crimean public voted overwhelmingly to leave Ukraine and re-join Russia.

The post-coup government dispatched newly recruited paramilitary National Guard units to assault the self-declared republics, with some units recruited from extreme right-wing groups that had provided the muscle for the coup against Yanukovych. NATO forces were soon training Ukrainian troops, including the neo-Nazi-led Azov Regiment, on how to operate new grenade launchers and other U.S. weapons.

To stem the violence, France and Germany helped negotiate the Minsk II Peace Accords in 2015, but rather than push the peace process forward, the U.S. sent Ukraine $75 million in "non-lethal" military aid and dispatched 300 military trainers to train Ukrainian National Guard units in "war-fighting functions" at the Yavoriv base. The Americans were soon joined by 200 Canadian and 75 British trainers.[7]

Yavoriv became the headquarters of the U.S. 7th Army Training Command, and troops from many NATO countries were deployed there, training up to 10,000 Ukrainian troops per year. NATO also provided funding, instructors, and advisers for the nearby National Army Academy in Lviv.[8] French and German leaders later admitted that they used the Minsk agreements to "buy time" to arm and train Ukraine.[9]

In 2019, a Ukrainian watchdog group reported that the U.S. had supplied 90% of the foreign military aid sent to Ukraine since 2014.[10] But as in Yugoslavia in the 1990s, NATO's role as a junior partner alongside the United States put a European face on the conflict. It also locked NATO members into a U.S. policy of preparing the Ukrainian military for war with Russia, instead of resolving the crisis peacefully by fulfilling the terms of the Minsk II Peace Accords.[11]

After the February 2022 Russian invasion, most NATO forces were withdrawn from Ukraine but NATO increased its training and education of Ukrainian forces in NATO countries. One of the problems with the training was the infiltration of extremist right-wing groups linked to Ukraine's Azov Regiment, which the U.S. Congress had by then prohibited funding, training, or provision of weapons because of its neo-Nazi ideology.[12]

Another problem was that the combat experience of U.S. and NATO troops in Iraq and Afghanistan was very different from the combat the Ukrainians faced, and their training ill-prepared Ukrainians for fighting heavily armed, technologically advanced Russian forces in open terrain or trench warfare, under heavy artillery bombardment, and without the air cover that U.S. forces take for granted.

So despite Ukraine's impressive initial gains soon after the Russian invasion, and despite all the training, intelligence support, and tens of billions of dollars worth of newly delivered U.S. and NATO weapons, the war in Ukraine eventually descended into a long, bloody war of attrition.

No Strategy Beyond Further Escalation

While the war in Ukraine has served to unite NATO members, it has united them behind a war policy that has been dictated by the United States and Britain—a war policy that nixed a solution that was actually within reach just one month after the invasion.

In late March 2022, thanks to peace talks mediated by Turkey, Russia was ready to withdraw from all the territory it had just occupied in return for a simple commitment by Ukraine to give up its ambition to join NATO and not to allow NATO military bases or missile installations on its territory. Ukrainian President Volodymyr Zelensky was ready to accept.

But then, on April 9, 2022, UK Prime Minister Boris Johnson flew into Kyiv and told Zelensky that the "collective West" would not support the agreement—and the talks ended. Germany, France, and Italy eventually fell in line behind the U.S. and the UK, as did Zelensky.

In late 2023, Russia reportedly proposed new peace negotiations—this time with the United States, knowing that the U.S. had pushed Ukraine not to negotiate.[13] Reuters broke the story of the Russian initiative, but reported that, after a meeting of intermediaries in Turkey, followed by a meeting in Washington with top U.S. officials, the U.S. quashed the idea. National Security Adviser Jake Sullivan told Putin's foreign policy adviser Yuri Ushakov that the U.S. was willing to talk to Russia about other matters, but not about peace in Ukraine.

These tensions are gradually exacerbating what has always been NATO's greatest weakness, that its purpose is to unite Europe under U.S. military leadership in a way that neither the U.S. nor the European public really supports. NATO has failed to unite the 32 countries and Ukraine behind any realistic war strategy. Instead it has rejected peace proposals coming from all over the world, including from African leaders, Latin American presidents, the Pope, and the Chinese government.

As this war of attrition rages on, the threat of a broader war between NATO and Russia looms. When NATO Secretary General Jens Stoltenberg revealed his greatest fear about the war in a TV interview in January 2023, he said it was that the fighting in Ukraine could spin out of control into a major war between NATO and Russia. "If things go wrong," he cautioned solemnly, "they can go horribly wrong."[14] Stoltenberg maintained that NATO was "working every day" to avoid a major war between NATO and Russia, but that such a war was a real possibility.

Concerned about a Ukrainian defeat, in February 2024, French President Macron proposed the idea of sending more NATO troops into Ukraine. His proposal was immediately shot down by other NATO members, but may well come to pass if it becomes clear that Ukraine is losing the war. Direct involvement of NATO troops could lead to World War III, even a nuclear war—the very catastrophic scenario that President Biden promised to avoid when the war began in 2022.[15]

In February 2024, the European Union approved an enormous $54 billion package of funding for Ukraine. In the U.S., as of this writing, President Biden's request for $60 billion (mostly for weapons) has been held up by political infighting. But while NATO leaders are trying to make an open-ended commitment to Ukraine, the enthusiastic support Ukrainians once received from the U.S. and European public has been replaced by war fatigue. This is especially true in the United States, where buying weapons for Ukraine has been opposed by Donald Trump and seen by many as a problem that Europeans should solve.

As the death toll continues to rise with no end in sight, perhaps our leaders should stop to think about a saying by the ancient Chinese philosopher Lao Tzu: "If you don't change direction, you may end up where you are heading."

5

NATO "Partners" Around the Globe

Article 10 of the North Atlantic Treaty limits new members of NATO to European nations that are invited by NATO to join it. But NATO has not limited itself to Europe. It does not view its purpose as merely "resisting armed attack" (in the language of that treaty). Not only has it reconceived the concept of resisting actual attacks as deterring potential attacks—often through behavior that is clearly more provocative than deterrent—but NATO also conceives of itself as a global alliance that will wage wars anywhere on Earth, regardless of any attack on a NATO member.

Outside of Europe, therefore, NATO has added dozens of additional nations as "partners" rather than members. To invite a nation to be a member, existing members must agree that, according to Article 5, an attack on one is an attack on all. To add a "partner," however, no such commitment is required. NATO may very well go to war in the event that one of its partners goes to war, but it is not obliged to by treaty.

NATO partners Armenia and Azerbaijan have been engaged in armed attacks on each other. Were they members instead of partners, NATO would be obliged to either support both sides or, more likely, declare one side to be in the wrong and wage war for the other.

Each partnership agreement is specific to the nation, and can be frequently modified to expand the partnership. A key concept for NATO partnerships is "interoperability." This means partners buying the same weapons, relying on the same people to maintain and repair and upgrade those weapons, relying on the same people to train military personnel on those weapons, and organizing militaries to function under the same command. The interoperability of partners, like members, is tested in "war games" or rehearsals, and in actual wars. NATO partner militaries have joined in its wars in Afghanistan and Libya, in patrolling the Mediterranean, in training (and making more interoperable) the Iraqi military, and in NATO's military occupation of Kosovo, which has never ended since NATO's war there in 1999. The permanent presence in Kosovo has long served as an initial training ground for the integration of new partners' militaries into NATO. Over the course of the 2001-2021 war in Afghanistan, 52 nations took part, including many NATO partners.

NATO partnership involves encouragement to spend more on militarism, to buy more weapons, and to engage in more military training and military strategizing. NATO trains thousands of partner-nation officials, both military and civilian, in militarized thinking through some 30 national "Partnership Training and Education Centres," and institutions like the NATO School in Oberammergau, Germany, and the NATO Defense College in Rome, Italy.

Who are NATO partners in Europe and Central Asia?

Partnership has, among other things, been a tool through which NATO has moved European nations toward membership and extended NATO's reach toward the border of Russia. Nations that first became partners of NATO and later members include the Czech Republic, Hungary, and Poland (1999); Bulgaria, Estonia, Latvia, Lithuania, Romania, Slovakia, and Slovenia (2004); Albania, Croatia, Montenegro, North Macedonia, Finland, and Sweden (between 2009 and 2024).

Present-day NATO partners in Europe, about which there has been a great deal of discussion regarding moving toward membership, include Ukraine and Georgia. Other partners that move NATO's reach eastward are Armenia, Azerbaijan, Kazakhstan, Kyrgyz Republic, Republic of Moldova, Tajikistan, Turkmenistan, and Uzbekistan. These nations were all once part of the Soviet Union. Their participation in the NATO alliance, from the perspective of the Russian government, is probably not entirely unlike how the U.S. government would perceive the independence of its states that were once part of Mexico, and their partnership in a hostile Mexican military alliance.

Other NATO partners in Europe are Austria, Bosnia and Herzegovina, Ireland, Malta, Serbia, and Switzerland. Some of these, like Sweden and Finland until just recently, are nations with traditions of (and in some cases constitutions requiring) neutrality. These nations resist the idea of full NATO membership, oftentimes because of popular opposition, but have welcomed collaboration with NATO through "partnership."

All of the current European partners are included in what NATO calls, perhaps in tribute to George Orwell, its Partnership for Peace, which was first created in 1994. A number of these same nations have been the sites of U.S.-supported "color revolutions," including Serbia in 2000, Georgia in 2003, Ukraine in 2004 (and again in 2014), Kyrgyz Republic in 2005, Moldova in 2005, and Armenia in 2018. These were often largely nonviolent revolutions drawing on the sincere support of people with legitimate grievances against abusive governments, but with various degrees of U.S. involvement aimed at moving nations closer to NATO and farther from Russia.

For some nations anxious to join the European Union, NATO partnership, followed by NATO membership, has looked like a path toward that more exclusive European Union club. Croatia became a NATO member in 2009 and a European Union member in 2013. Romania and Bulgaria became NATO members in 2004 and European Union members in 2007. Slovenia and Slovakia joined both NATO and the EU in 2004 after NATO partnerships, as did Lithuania, Latvia, and Estonia. Poland became a NATO member in 1999 and an EU member in 2004, as did Hungary and the Czech Republic, all following NATO partnerships. Malta became a NATO partner in 1995 and an EU member in 2004.

The partnerships with Ukraine and Georgia have been the most dangerous in terms of U.S.-Russia relations. NATO has declared its intention to someday make both nations members. Russia has threatened war over either move. Yet NATO has pressed ahead, including Georgian troops in its patrols of the Mediterranean, supporting war in eastern Ukraine between 2014 and 2022, and supporting the war against the Russian invasion since then.

The two oddest members of NATO's "Partnership for Peace," however, are Russia and Belarus. Both of those nations' memberships have been "suspended" by NATO. The partnership with Russia was always fraught. While the Soviet Union had been an ally of the United States in World War II, its request to join NATO in 1954 was rejected.[1]

NATO (which then had merely 14 members and no partners) also rejected a proposal for a new alliance that would
include the Soviet Union, arguing that any alliance so large
would be a threat to the United Nations. (So what is NATO
now?) Scholars have concluded that the United States
never even considered making Russia a NATO member,
because it never believed Russia would subordinate itself
to U.S. leadership.[2]

Russian President Vladimir Putin reportedly asked
to join NATO as recently as 2000.[3] It is hard to believe
NATO's rejection was motivated solely by Putin demand-
ing to be invited rather than humbly applying to join. For
one thing, NATO has gone out of its way to court potential members. For another, NATO's statements on its purpose, its very reason for existence, have for years focused
largely on the threat of Russia. Within the U.S. military,
overhyping the supposed threat of Russia has long been
a top means of increasing military spending, as U.S. military officials have confessed to journalists.[4]

Which countries are NATO partners in Western Asia and North Africa?

Always viewing militarism as the answer to the problems
it creates, NATO has established partnerships across the
region that have wreaked havoc, spreading weaponry
and instability.

One initiative, the Mediterranean Dialogue, includes Algeria, Egypt, Israel, Jordan, Mauritania, Morocco, and Tunisia. Another, the Istanbul Cooperation Initiative, includes Bahrain, Kuwait, Qatar, and the United Arab Emirates. In addition, through what NATO calls "Partners Across the Globe," NATO has established partnerships with Iraq, Pakistan, and Afghanistan.

These NATO partners include some of the most oppressive, authoritarian and dictatorial governments, deemed the least "free" by the U.S.-funded Freedom House rankings,[5] and considered by the U.S. Department of State responsible for all variety of brutal human rights abuses.[6] NATO has probably sacrificed entire forests, not just to the war in Afghanistan, but to the publication of reports on how its mission is spreading democracy and freedom—as well as defending the world from just the sort of governments that in reality it militarizes and trains through these partnerships.

In 2005, NATO began collaborating with the militaries of the 55-member-nation African Union. NATO maintains liaison offices to the African Union.

What about NATO partners in other parts of the world?

Additional NATO partners around the world include Mongolia, the Republic of Korea, Japan, Australia, New Zealand, and Colombia. NATO is a global enterprise.

That is evident both from this list of partners and from NATO's discussions of its goals and missions, including its growing obsession with China as an economic/military enemy (the line between the two is energetically blurred).

NATO has also involved the Philippines in war rehearsals.[7]

In 2014, NATO created something called "Enhanced Opportunity Partner Status" and bestowed it on Australia, Finland, Georgia, Jordan, and Sweden. In 2020 it added Ukraine. NATO describes this status as including:

- "regular, political consultations on security matters, including possibly at ministerial level;
- enhanced access to interoperability programmes and exercises;
- sharing information, including on lessons learned;
- closer association of such partners in times of crisis and the preparation of operations."[8]

This status also appears to be a step toward membership, as two of the six Enhanced Opportunity Partners have become members (Finland and Sweden) and another two are widely discussed as possible members (Ukraine and Georgia).

In 2021, two NATO members, the U.S. and UK, and NATO partner Australia formed AUKUS, a pact primarily focused on military cooperation in the Indo-Pacific region. A key component of AUKUS is Australia's acquisition of nuclear-powered submarines, leveraging technology provided by the U.S. and the UK (rather than France or any other weapons dealer). New Zealand is considering membership.

AUKUS introduces nuclear-powered submarines to a region of the world where the U.S. government—with the aid of its allies and weapons customers—has long been engaged in provoking conflict with China. This could fuel an arms race, the further militarization of Australia, and the further incorporation of Australia into a global U.S. military. The arms race could, of course, lead to actual war.

In 2020, a NATO report called "NATO 2030" recommended that NATO "expand and strengthen partnerships with Ukraine and Georgia, seek to heighten engagement with Bosnia and Herzegovina, and counter destabilisation across the Western Balkans. NATO should energise the Mediterranean Dialogue (MD) and the Istanbul Cooperation Initiative (ICI) through strengthened political engagement, capacity building, and resilience enhancement. It should deepen cooperation with Indo-Pacific partners."[9]

In 2020 NATO also issued a proclamation that included as NATO priorities: "a. to stress that NATO can contribute to both Euro-Atlantic and global security by working hand-in-hand with, and building the capacity of, its partners around the world; . . . d. to ensure the fullest involvement of non-EU Allied countries in efforts to enhance European security and defence in the spirit of full mutual openness and in compliance with the decision-making autonomy and procedures of the two organisations; e. to continue to develop political and practical cooperation with the United Nations, the OSCE, the Council of Europe, the African Union, the Arab League, the Gulf Cooperation Council, and other relevant international organisations; f. to establish a NATO-certified Centre of Excellence on the Indo-Pacific region."[10]

When looking at NATO's global reach, we cannot forget the role of the vast network of U.S. military bases around the world. The U.S. has more than 900 overseas bases, and at least 56 of them are used by NATO. These NATO bases are found in Belgium, Bulgaria, Estonia, Georgia, Germany, Greece, Greenland, Hungary, Iceland, Italy, Latvia, the Netherlands, Norway, Poland, Portugal, Romania, Spain, Turkey, and the United Kingdom. Those are all NATO members except Georgia.

Are NATO partners also weapons partners?

If you take the list of 66 NATO members and partners, and a list of about the same number of nations that imported U.S. weapons between 2014 and 2022,[11] the two lists would be remarkably similar. In fact, 54 of the NATO members and partners (or 82%) are also U.S. weapons customers. While other NATO countries export weapons—all NATO countries combine for about 65% of worldwide arms exports—the largest exporter by far is the United States, accounting for 42% of global exports.[12]

The initiation of U.S. weapons sales has followed NATO partnership and membership far more reliably than has EU membership or the flourishing of democracy. The boost given to NATO by the current war in Ukraine has included not only new members, but many new U.S. weapons sales, and a greatly strengthened push for NATO members to spend more on weapons.

While NATO is thought of as an alliance of existing militaries, it also expends much of its energy on the NATO Support and Procurement Agency, which lines up weapons deals between manufacturers and governments. The NATO Support and Procurement Agency is headquartered in Luxembourg with "operational centers" in France, Hungary, and Italy. It has a greater number of staff and handles greater amounts of money than does NATO itself. According to NATO's 2023 annual report, NATO's international staff consisted of 1,352 civilians, but the NATO Support and Procurement Agency employed "more than 1,400 international civilian personnel" and in 2023, "the value of the Agency's business activity exceeded EUR 5 billion," which is greater than NATO's total budget.

NATO also raises money from its partners to spend on weapons. In January 2024, the prime minister of Japan committed $37 million to NATO for the purpose of buying weapons for Ukraine.[13] NATO also talks about building more relationships with "the private sector."[14]

With all of these "partnerships," NATO is a global weapons behemoth. The U.S. military alone dwarfs the rest of the world, but adding NATO members and partners makes it significantly larger. In military spending, out of 230 other countries, the U.S. spends more than all but three of them combined.[15] NATO members and partners together account for 69% of the world's military spending. China spends 19% what NATO members and partners do. Russia spends 6% what NATO members and partners do. Iran spends 0.4% what NATO members and partners do.

What are Israel's relations with NATO?

In 2017, Israel established a permanent and official mission to NATO headquarters and there have been efforts over the years to integrate Israel more closely into NATO to take advantage of its advanced weapons systems.[16]

But NATO countries have been supporting Israel since its creation by funding, arming, and training the Israeli military and providing diplomatic cover for Israel's crimes.

For decades, there has been close coordination between Israel and the weapons industries of NATO members. NATO members have purchased billions in weapons—weapons that have been field-tested in Gaza. These range from the Arrow 3 missile defense system (sold to Germany for $3.5 billion) to "Kamikaze drones" and counter-drone systems. Israeli weapons exports soared after Russia's 2022 invasion, when NATO members became more anxious to learn about, and purchase, Israel's advanced military technology.

NATO is particularly interested in Israel's use of artificial intelligence (AI), which began with Israel's attack on Gaza in 2021 but became a key component of its military strategy after October 7, 2023. In Israel's targeting of Palestinians, the army used an artificial intelligence-based program known as "Lavender," which played a central role in the bombing that killed tens of thousands of people in Gaza.[17]

Israeli military officials have briefed NATO on Israel's "innovations," and Israel's President Isaac Herzog visited NATO headquarters in 2023—the first time an Israeli president has addressed NATO allies there. NATO and the Israeli government have also been in communication about what they consider threats from Iran.

But after Israel's genocidal response to the October 7, 2023 Hamas attack, divisions within NATO began to emerge. All NATO members condemned the attack and

NATO Secretary General Jens Stoltenberg asserted that "Israel does not stand alone."[18] But as the months went on and the gruesome death toll mounted, countries reacted differently. Some, such as the United States, the Czech Republic, Hungary, and Germany, staunchly stood by Israel; others, such as Belgium, Spain, and Slovenia, expressed sympathy for the plight of the Palestinians.

An early sign of division appeared during the December 2023 UN General Assembly vote on a cease-fire resolution. The resolution passed overwhelmingly with 153 countries in favor, including most NATO members. But among the 10 nations that voted "No" were two NATO members: the United States and the Czech Republic. The 23 nations that abstained included NATO members Germany, Hungary, Italy, the Netherlands, and the UK.

Also in December 2023, when U.S. Defense Secretary Lloyd Austin announced the creation of a naval group to prevent Houthi attacks on ships traveling in the Red Sea, attacks that were in response to Israel's slaughter in Gaza, only a few European nations signed the joint statement and even fewer agreed to participate in efforts to attack the Houthis. Some, like France, expressed preference for an autonomous, European-led operation.[19] Still others, like Spain, were skeptical of any involvement in any anti-Houthi action whatsoever.[20]

NATO members were divided over whether or not to keep sending weapons to Israel. On February 12, 2024, responding to a remark by President Biden that Israel's attacks on Gaza were "over the top," European Union foreign policy chief Josep Borrell commented, "Well, if you believe that too many people are being killed, maybe you should provide less arms in order to prevent so many people being killed."[21]

Indeed, for years, the United States has accounted for almost 70% of Israel's arms imports and has continued to send weapons during the massacre. Other nations have had robust discussions in their assemblies and have banned arms shipments to Israel. These include NATO members Canada, Spain, the Netherlands, and Belgium.

Even the issue of humanitarian aid was contentious, particularly the funding for the UN Relief and Works Agency (UNRWA), the principal humanitarian agency in Palestine. When Israel made the unsubstantiated accusation that 12 of UNRWA's 13,000 Gaza staff members participated in the October 7 attack, more than a dozen countries, including the United States and several other NATO members, suspended funding. Others, like France and Germany, said they'd wait for the results of the investigations,[22] and still others, like Denmark, Belgium, Luxembourg, Spain, and Slovenia, pledged to continue the funding. Spain actually tripled its contribution and the EU's Josep Borrell warned that defunding UNRWA would be "disproportionate and dangerous," amounting to a form of collective punishment of Palestinian civilians.[23]

As of this writing, the outcome and impact of the Israel/Palestine conflict is still unclear. What is clear, however, is that the idea of a warmer Israel/NATO embrace has been put on ice.

6

Who Makes the Decisions
And Who Pays?

As self-appointed global defender of democracy, the "free world," and the "Rules-Based Order," NATO makes its own decisions without any public referenda, separate from any elected governments, with no recorded votes, behind closed doors, and outside the structure of the United Nations, which did not authorize the wars in Yugoslavia, Afghanistan or Libya. With regard to Libya, the UN authorized a rescue mission, not a war or a government overthrow. NATO's secretive decision-making is at odds with the fact that NATO trains government officials around the world in what it calls "integrity, transparency, and accountability" and has bragged about training 800 Ukrainians in 2023 in how to not be corrupt.[1]

What we know of NATO meetings behind closed doors, and what we see out in the open, suggests a general answer to the question of who decides what NATO does. The answer is, for the most part: the U.S. government. Europe may have a larger economy than the United States and may surpass the United States in all kinds of measures of health and well-being, but when it comes to militaries, the U.S. military is much larger than all of the other NATO militaries combined. The U.S. military has troops in every nation in Europe, including major bases in several of them, none of which has a single base in the United States. Without the United States, NATO would be nonexistent or unrecognizable.

A key example of U.S. dominance is that, although there have been foreign terrorist incidents in most or all NATO member nations, only once has one of them been called an "armed attack" that required all other NATO member nations to take action (mostly by joining in a war). That was after the September 11, 2001, crimes in the United States. Following secret briefings by U.S. officials, NATO complied with the U.S. request to invoke Article 5, leading to the horrific and catastrophic NATO war in Afghanistan.

An incident from 2003 is also telling about the dominant U.S. role. There were moves in a Belgian court to prosecute General Tommy Franks, the commander of the U.S. troops in Iraq, for using cluster bombs in civilian areas in Iraq.[2] U.S. Secretary of Defense Donald Rumsfeld dealt with that problem at a NATO meeting by warning

Belgium that the United States would not fund NATO's headquarters in Belgium, and would not take part in meetings in Belgium, leaving the impression that NATO headquarters would be moved elsewhere. The prosecution quickly disappeared, while the war on Iraq rolled on unchanged.[3]

There have been only 13 Secretaries General of NATO, one of whom (Willy Claes) served only a year because it was discovered he had previously taken a large bribe from a weapons dealer. The secretaries general have all been chosen by the "consensus" of NATO members. In those cases where we know which nations first backed a nomination, these nominees have always had early backing from the U.S. government. On some occasions, carrots and sticks used to achieve "consensus"— the sorts of things not allowed in actually democratic voting in a free world—have been made public. When Turkey objected to Anders Fogh Rasmussen as Secretary General, Turkey backed down after a deal was made to shut down an international television network disliked by the Turkish government (Roj TV).

As we were writing this book, the U.S. government had backed the outgoing Dutch Prime Minister as the next Secretary General of NATO. The President of Romania declared himself a candidate, but it is hard to imagine his campaign succeeding without U.S. support.[4] His reported consent for NATO to build a new base in Romania, allegedly its largest in all of Europe, may indeed win him U.S. support.[5]

The Secretary General oversees a staff of 1,352 people and chairs the North Atlantic Council, which is made up of delegates from each NATO member nation—delegates elected by no one but empowered by their governments to make decisions on the use of militaries and on the spending of money. The North Atlantic Council, the main body of NATO, should not be confused with the Atlantic Council, a U.S. "think tank" with a revolving door into the U.S. government and funding from weapons companies and governments the world over.

How do the NATO committees function?

NATO has 21 committees that report to the North Atlantic Council. Some are considered so important that they are not subsidiary to the North Atlantic Council but on its level. One of them is the Nuclear Planning Committee, which is chaired by the Secretary General and handles NATO's nuclear policies (see chapter on nuclear weapons below). The other is the Military Committee, which both advises the North Atlantic Council and instructs or "gives guidance to" NATO's military commanders. It also engages with NATO partners.

The Chair of the NATO Military Committee is elected from among the so-called chiefs of "defense" of NATO member nations. In the United States, for example, this is the Chairman of the Joint Chiefs of Staff. But the Chair of the Military Committee is understood to be a non-U.S. chief. The current one is Admiral Rob Bauer of the Royal Netherlands Navy.

The NATO Military Committee communicates NATO's decisions to two military commanders who are somehow both "supreme." One is the Supreme Allied Commander Europe. The current one is the 20th, and all 20 have been from the United States. The Supreme Allied Commander Europe is, in fact, also simultaneously the Commander of the United States European Command. Given the U.S. government's long-standing opposition to U.S. troops following orders given by a non-U.S. commander, the lead commander in Europe pretty well has to be from the U.S. Every NATO member nation is required to serve under U.S. command during NATO wars, whereas the U.S. military has never agreed to obey any other nation's command.

The second supreme military commander has been given the odd name of the Supreme Allied Commander Transformation. The Allied Command Transformation is based in Norfolk, Virginia, home of the world's largest naval base, but its mission is not NATO military operations. Rather it is tasked with transforming NATO. Part of what "transforming" NATO seems to mean is expanding NATO from an institution for defending Europe against a military attack into an institution for policing the globe in pursuit of terrorism, human/drug smuggling, piracy, and espionage. A U.S. admiral and two U.S. generals held the position of Supreme Allied Commander Transformation from 2003 to 2009, since which date it has been held by generals in the French Air Force.

Who pays for NATO?

The topic of who pays for NATO has been featured in U.S. media in recent years because of the numerous comments by Donald Trump, including his claimed remarks to a leader of a NATO member nation: "You didn't pay? You're delinquent? . . . No I would not protect you, in fact I would encourage them to do whatever they want. You gotta pay."[6] This was widely, and pretty fairly, reported as Trump encouraging Russia to attack a NATO country if it did not pay its dues to NATO.[7] A bit less fairly, Trump's remarks have been described by President Joe Biden as "bowing down to Putin." Missing in the reporting of Trump's hideously murderous remarks is a clear understanding of how NATO funding works, including an explanation of why "delinquency" and "paying dues" are thoroughly misleading concepts here.

NATO's annual budget is about $3.6 billion. That sounds like a lot of money to normal people, but in the world of weaponry and militaries, it is a rounding error. Media chatter about "paying into NATO" is misleading because the real issue is not NATO's budget, which all NATO members have been paying into. It is about how much money each country is spending on its own military.

In a totally undemocratic fashion in 2006, without a vote by elected governments—much less the consent of the taxpayers in their countries—NATO Defense Ministers got together and decided that all members should commit a minimum of 2% of their nations' Gross Domestic Product (GDP) to military spending so that they could "continue to ensure the Alliance's military readiness." This guideline, they said, also "serves as an indicator of a country's political will to contribute to NATO's common defence efforts, since the defence capacity of each member has an impact on the overall perception of the Alliance's credibility as a politico-military organisation."[8] In 2014, this 2% minimum was confirmed by NATO heads of state, with the goal that all members would meet this target by 2024 and that at least 20% of their nations' military spending would go to "major equipment" (weapons). In 2014, only three countries were meeting the 2% goal; by 2023, that number had risen to 24. The U.S., spending 3.5% of GDP on the military, far surpassed the "goal."

NATO (and Biden and Trump and Obama and weapons-funded think tanks and all variety of U.S. pundits) want NATO members to spend more on militaries, and have determined that the best way to do this is to treat militarism as a public good without limit, to be measured as a percentage of growing economies.

There are all kinds of problems with this. If you clear a pristine forest for a military training ground, your nation becomes uglier and your ecosystem weaker, but your "economy" larger, meaning that you should now spend more money on your military to maintain a proper percentage of your economy going into the war machine.

Another problem is that 2% of GDP sounds like a small contribution, making it more palatable to the public. But GDP measures the monetary value of ALL goods and services produced within a country's borders for an entire year, and 2% of that is actually enormous.

Military spending can be, and used to be, measured in absolute dollar amounts. The trouble with that, for those who want to see more and more gargantuan piles of wealth being dumped into war preparation, is that the public can see the enormous numbers and compare them with spending on areas they might like better—such as spending on healthcare, green jobs, education, you name it. "A trillion dollars," which is what the U.S. now spends on militarism, sounds a lot more ominous than 3.5% of GDP.

When it comes to pushing NATO members to boost their military spending, the Russian invasion of Ukraine has done far more than Trump's rhetoric. According to

NATO's 2023 annual report, in 2023 military spending "increased by an unprecedented 11% across Europe and Canada," despite having also increased in each of the previous eight years. And in 2024, "we expect two-thirds of Allies to meet or exceed the target of investing 2% of Gross Domestic Product" in militarism. NATO falsely claims in the same report that all this military spending will mean "more highly skilled jobs across Europe and North America," even though studies have actually found that military spending reduces jobs compared with non-military spending or never taxing the money from working people in the first place.[9]

Across the political spectrum of the U.S. establishment, it is widely believed that European nations are morally failing by not further increasing their military spending as a service to the world and as protection of themselves. Here is a tweet from liberal professor and author Stephen Wertheim:

"European allies have had eight years since 2016 to bolster their defenses in light of the fact that the leader of one of the two American political parties does not want to come to the defense of NATO allies. They remain long on denunciations, short on actions."[10]

The possibility that some Europeans are not war-crazed maniacs who are freeloading, but rather are people prioritizing spending to address climate, disease, homelessness and poverty is literally unthinkable on this side of the pond. Yet such prioritization is articulated by various European politicians and does not sound insane. In fact, it is very popular among the public.

Military spending famously requires enormous trade-offs. It would cost about 3% of U.S. military spending to end starvation on Earth, a bit over 1% to provide the world with clean drinking water, about 7% to end poverty in the United States, and other small fractions to transform education or green energy.[11] Prioritizing bringing military spending up to levels decreed by a club of militaries and never put to a public or even a congressional/parliamentary vote anywhere is a choice, but it is not the only choice. And it is not the only way imaginable to advance "freedom" or "democracy."

7

How Does NATO Relate to the UN and International Law?

In typical U.S. discourse, for one nation to launch a big new war alone is reckless and rogue. But for a big coalition of nations to begin bombing another country together is responsible global citizenship. Be that as it may, we should be clear that neither type of action is any more or less legal than the other. If attacking Yugoslavia or Afghanistan or Libya is illegal, then it remains illegal even if you bring together a big gang of governments to do it with you. It is a crime for someone to rob the corner grocery store, whether alone or with a big group of friends. And it is generally a crime to launch a war no matter who helps you do it.

Since 1899, all parties to the Convention for the Pacific Settlement of International Disputes have committed that they "agree to use their best efforts to insure the pacific settlement of international differences."

Since 1907, all parties to the Hague Convention of 1907 have been obliged to "use their best efforts to ensure the pacific settlement of international differences," to appeal to other nations to mediate, to accept offers of mediation from other nations, to create if needed "an International Commission of Inquiry, to facilitate a solution of these disputes by elucidating the facts by means of an impartial and conscientious investigation," and to appeal if needed to the permanent court at The Hague for arbitration.

Since 1928, all parties to the Kellogg-Briand Pact (currently 66 nations) have been legally required to "condemn recourse to war for the solution of international controversies, and renounce it, as an instrument of national policy in their relations with one another," and to "agree that the settlement or solution of all disputes or conflicts of whatever nature or of whatever origin they may be, which may arise among them, shall never be sought except by pacific means."

Since 1945, all parties to the United Nations Charter have been compelled to "settle their international disputes by peaceful means in such a manner that international peace and security, and justice, are not endangered," and to "refrain in their international relations from the threat or use of force against the territorial integrity or political independence of any state," albeit with loopholes added for UN-authorized wars and wars of "self-defense." The requirement of peace and ban on war or the threat of war has been elaborated over the years in various UN resolutions, such as 2625 and 3314, as well as in the ANZUS Treaty, the Treaty of Amity and Cooperation in Southeast Asia, the Community of Latin American and Caribbean States' Declaration of a Zone of Peace, and even the opening words of the North Atlantic Treaty that created NATO.

Since 1976, the International Covenant on Civil and Political Rights (ICCPR) and the International Covenant on Economic, Social, and Cultural Rights have bound their parties to these opening words of Article I of both treaties: "All peoples have the right of self-determination." The same ICCPR requires that "Any propaganda for war shall be prohibited by law." NATO's wars, and NATO's communications about its wars, violate these treaties. Or, rather, NATO's member states and partner states violate these international laws. NATO itself is not a nation and not a party to treaties. A case must be brought to the International Court of Justice against a nation. But cases can be prosecuted by the International Criminal Court against individuals, although thus far all individuals prosecuted have been from Africa and none from NATO or even NATO member or partner nations. That biased use of the court has a lot to do with NATO's dominant member, the U.S. government.

Is the United States outside the law?

The United States has an odd relationship to international law. Of 18 major human rights treaties, the United States is party to only five, as few as any nation on Earth. The U.S. government is a leading holdout on disarmament treaties, disregards the rulings of the International Court of Justice, refuses to join the International Criminal Court, and punishes other nations for doing so—and even sanctioned officers of the court to dissuade them from doing their jobs. It has brought pressure on the Spanish and Belgian governments when their courts have sought to prosecute U.S. crimes. It has spied on and bribed other members of the United Nations to influence votes. (It has similarly bribed other members of NATO to achieve "consensus," but that practice is hardly even thought of as illicit.)

It has interfered in elections and facilitated coups. It employs massive and unaccountable secret agencies. It engages in assassinations. It claims the right to blow up anyone, anywhere with missiles from robotic airplanes. It sabotages pipelines and other infrastructure, heedless of the law or the damage done. It opposes new treaties almost universally, including those proposed to ban the weaponization of space, cyber attacks, and nuclear weapons. And yet, both the United States and NATO talk endlessly about supporting "the Rules-Based Order."

One key reason why there is no universal Rules-Based Order is the veto at the UN Security Council. Since 1972, the U.S. government has been far and away the leading user of the veto, often blocking the will of every, or nearly every, other national government on Earth. It has vetoed UN condemnation of South African apartheid, Israel's wars and occupations, chemical and biological weapons, nuclear weapons proliferation, first use of nuclear weapons and use against non-nuclear nations, U.S. wars in Nicaragua and Grenada and Panama, the U.S. embargo on Cuba, Rwandan genocide, the deployment of weapons in outer space, and much more. Dozens of times, the U.S. has vetoed steps toward peace or justice in Palestine. And this is just scraping the surface. The primary use of the veto power is as an unrecorded threat of a veto made behind closed doors to keep many undesired topics off the public agenda entirely.

Another large gap in the Rules-Based Order is created by sanctions of the sort employed by the U.S. government and NATO. Sanctions authorized by the United Nations and not punishing a whole population, but rather targeting powerful individuals guilty of major crimes, are legal. The U.S. government, however, uses unilateral sanctions to punish entire populations (or to coerce other governments to join in punishing entire populations). Such sanctions violate national sovereignty and bans on collective punishment in the Geneva Conventions as well as the UN Charter, the International Covenant on Civil and Political Rights, and in some cases the Genocide Convention. When NATO joins in these efforts it does nothing to legalize them.

The U.S. government uses sanctions as a step toward war (as in Iraq) or as a step toward weakening or overthrowing a government (as in Russia).[1] The U.S. government has been asked but has refused to say what its sanctions on dozens of governments accomplish.[2] Clearly, if nothing else, they cause tremendous human suffering. The U.S. government has imposed brutal sanctions against many non-NATO governments, sanctions that hit the populations in a purported effort to alter or overturn the governments that the U.S. government does not like for whatever reasons. When NATO assists in these efforts, it serves as an accomplice, not a justification.

The NATO Article 5 commitment to join in others' wars has a precedent in the treaties that created, or were used to create, the First World War. Britain cited the 1839 Treaty of London as a basis for joining the war in support of Belgium. And both world wars were precedents for nations joining in others' wars, whether obliged to do so or not. But the precedent of the First World War especially was deeply and widely regretted, and the idea of committing to join in others' unspecified future wars (no matter how defensive or humanitarian or noble) was not put to a public vote by any of the creators of NATO.

Importantly, World War I occurred before most of the laws against war were in place. War was generally thought of as legal, or as existing outside the realm of law. So it was arguably not illegal to commit to joining in another nation's war. But what about now? Even if you argue for the loopholes found in the UN Charter, and hypothesize a war that meets one or both of them, such a theoretically legal war would only be legal for the nation or nations that had been deemed to be fighting on the defensive side or for the nation or nations that had been authorized to wage war by the United Nations.

Is NATO even legal?

Article 5 of the North Atlantic Treaty declares that NATO members will assist another member if attacked by *"taking action as it deems necessary, including the use of armed force."* But the UN Charter does not say anywhere that warmaking is authorized for whoever jumps in on the appropriate side.

The North Atlantic Treaty's authors may have been aware that they were on dubious legal ground because they went on twice to claim otherwise, first adding the words "Any such armed attack and all measures taken as a result thereof shall immediately be reported to the Security Council. Such measures shall be terminated when the Security Council has taken the measures necessary to restore and maintain international peace and security." But shouldn't the United Nations be the one to decide when it has taken necessary measures and when it has not?

The North Atlantic Treaty adds a second bit of sham obsequiousness with the words "This Treaty does not affect, and shall not be interpreted as affecting in any way the rights and obligations under the Charter of the Parties which are members of the United Nations, or the primary responsibility of the Security Council for the maintenance of international peace and security." So the treaty seeks to obscure the fact that it is, indeed, authorizing warmaking outside of the United Nations.

Despite NATO's dubious legal standing, it actually serves in U.S. discourse as a legal justifier. When the U.S., UK, and three other nations attacked Yemen in January 2024, NATO helpfully published a statement declaring the action to have been "defensive."[3] If NATO and the United Nations are a bit conflated in your mind—they are both international and have something to do with war—this sounds like a judicial finding, whereas in reality it is simply a bit of rhetoric, eminently open to question, since interfering with shipping in waters near Yemen (the offense used as justification for the attacks) is not identical to launching a military attack on the United States and four other countries.

Also in January 2024, a Bosnian president appealed to NATO to wage war to prevent the secession of part of his country, illustrating not what NATO actually has a legal right to do, but what some people believe NATO can and will do.[4]

Despite NATO not being an elected body representative of or accountable to any public, it is used by the U.S. Congress as a means of shirking responsibility. The claim is frequently made that Congress need not investigate the atrocities of a war because it is a NATO war.

Despite NATO being dominated by the U.S. government, it is used in U.S. media to depict wars as carefully chosen rational actions of the "international community." That has long been a primary purpose the U.S. government has had for keeping NATO members in NATO and taking actions through NATO.

The more NATO becomes the entity that is understood to be taking actions in the world, rather than the U.S. military, the harder it is to oppose those actions. People cannot get upset with and vote out their local representative to NATO because there is no such thing. This is perhaps best illustrated by the following incident.

Since the 2022 Russian invasion of Ukraine, a great debate has raged between those who claim the invasion was "unprovoked" and those who—while condemning the invasion as a horrific, murderous crime—point out that it was just about the most openly and enduringly provoked attack in history, with Western officials warning of it or publicly advocating for it for years. The latter side of the debate has pointed to NATO expansion as central to the provocation.

But who would have expected the Secretary General of NATO himself, Jens Stoltenberg, to openly admit that it was NATO's expansion that led to the Russian invasion? In a talk on September 7, 2023, Stoltenberg said that, in the autumn of 2021, President Putin sent a draft treaty that he wanted NATO to sign, promising no more NATO enlargement. "It was a pre-condition for not invading Ukraine. Of course we didn't sign that," he said. "We rejected that. So he went to war to prevent NATO, more NATO, close to his borders."[5]

Were NATO's leader a national president, all hell would have broken loose with this admission. But he is merely the Secretary General of NATO, about whom the very idea of accountability does not seem to arise.

8

NATO and Nuclear Weapons

NATO calls itself a "nuclear alliance" and maintains a "Nuclear Planning Group" for all of its members—those with and those without nuclear weapons—to discuss the launching of the sort of war that puts all life on Earth at risk,[1] and to coordinate rehearsals or "war games" practicing for the use of nuclear weapons in Europe.[2]

NATO itself owns and controls no nuclear weapons. Three NATO members own and control nuclear weapons. We cannot be certain how many weapons they have, since nuclear weapons are both justified with the dubious alchemy of "deterrence" and, contradictorily, cloaked in secrecy. The United States has an estimated 5,344 nuclear weapons, France an estimated 290, and Great Britain an estimated 240.[3]

NATO partners Israel and Pakistan are estimated to possess 170 nuclear weapons each.

Five NATO members have U.S. nuclear weapons stored and controlled by the U.S. military within their borders: Belgium, Germany, Italy, the Netherlands and Turkey. These are estimated at 35 nuclear weapons at Aviano and Ghedi Air Bases in Italy, 20 at Incirlik in Turkey, and 15 each at Kleine Brogel in Belgium, Volkel Air Base in the Netherlands, and Büchel Air Base in Germany. The United States is reportedly also moving its own nuclear weapons into RAF Lakenheath in the UK, where it has stored them in the past.[4]

In recent years, the United States has been replacing its nuclear bombs stored in European nations with a newer model (the B61-12), while NATO members have been buying new U.S.-made airplanes with which to drop them.[5] Turkey has had U.S. nukes stored in it even while U.S.-backed and Turkish-backed troops have fought each other in Syria,[6] and even during a non-U.S.-backed coup attempt at the very base where the nuclear weapons are stored.[7]

Seven other NATO members are said to support "nuclear missions" using their non-nuclear militaries: The Czech Republic, Denmark, Greece, Hungary, Norway, Poland, and Romania.[8]

Poland and Romania also host new U.S./NATO missile bases that could launch missiles into Russia from very short distances, leaving the Russian government mere moments to decide whether the weapons are nuclear, or to decide whether to launch missiles of its own. The U.S. and NATO claim the bases are purely defensive, and various supporters of the bases have even claimed they had nothing to do with Russia—that they were either focused on Iran (then U.S. President Barack Obama)[9] or purely functioned as jobs programs for U.S. workers (former U.S. Ambassador Jack Matlock).[10]

Meanwhile, the U.S. has been manufacturing what many of its officials describe as "more usable" or "tactical" nuclear weapons (merely several times the destructive power of what was used on Hiroshima).[11] At the same time, the U.S. military is aware that, in its war game scenarios, the use of a single so-called "tactical" nuclear weapon tends to lead to all-out nuclear war. Or, as then Secretary of Defense Jim Mattis told the House Armed Services Committee in 2018, "I don't think there is any such thing as a 'tactical nuclear weapon.' Any nuclear weapon used any time is a strategic game-changer."[12]

The U.S.-made, disaster-prone F-35 is the first "stealth" airplane designed to carry nuclear bombs, meaning that it can in theory drop a nuclear bomb on a city with no warning from radar at all.[13] The U.S./NATO have managed to sell F-35s to the U.S., UK, Italy, Netherlands, Norway, Denmark, Belgium, Poland, Israel, Australia, Japan, South Korea, and Singapore, with efforts underway to spread them to more nations, eventually perhaps creating a general need for them on the grounds of "interoperability."

The U.S. military has enough nuclear weapons in each of the following three forms to threaten all life on our planet: missiles on U.S. submarines in oceans around the world; bombs on U.S. airplanes circling the globe; and missiles in the ground in the United States. So why also keep nuclear bombs in European countries, where they would have to be loaded onto airplanes and flown (presumably to Russia) on missions either so "stealth" that they avoid all warning or so risky that they would have to be preceded by massive efforts to destroy air defenses?

If the decision to "go nuclear" were up to NATO, all members would have to reach a consensus on it. However, NATO has not always easily reached a consensus. For example, the U.S. attempted to bring NATO into its plans for a war on Iraq in 2003 but failed, in part because of huge public pressure against that war in NATO nations. Nuclear war is one of the least popular ideas ever, so the launch of a nuclear weapon might have to be "stealth" not only in relation to Russia but also in relation to the Western public.[14] If the U.S. decides to use nuclear weapons, it almost certainly will not bother trying to use the ones it keeps stored in Europe. For that matter, were U.S. officials intent on reaching secret bunkers under hills some distance from Washington, D.C., they would need significant warning that a nuclear war had been secretly scheduled—a problematic concept for both the idea of deterrence and the idea of democracy.

Remember, the purpose of NATO in the North Atlantic Treaty is supposed to be defense against an attack on Europe, not deterrence. But in the event of responding to such an attack, whether the response were nuclear or not, the U.S. bombs stored in Europe would probably not be used. Threats in the name of deterrence have tended to fuel arms races and wars. But keeping U.S. nuclear weapons in Europe seems to fail even by the usual standards of deterrence theory, since their most likely use would be in an unlikely secret attack. Some U.S. officials believe those nuclear bombs serve no "military purpose" but only a "political" one, to reassure the host countries that the U.S. government cares about them.[15]

The argument has also been made that, since Russia would like the nuclear bombs removed from Europe, the U.S. should either keep them there or demand something huge from Russia in exchange for removing them.[16] Another argument is that this is part of making European nations share the burden, along the lines of making them spend more money on weapons. But if the burden serves no purpose, why should anyone share it? European government officials know the bombs are not useful as bombs. They know the bombs are provocative toward Russia. They know, in fact, that Russia is using the U.S. storage of nuclear bombs in European nations as an excuse to put Russian nuclear weapons into Belarus. The Russian Ambassador to the United States recently told David Swanson that Russia had every right to put nuclear weapons in Belarus because of the U.S. practice of storing them in other countries.

So a more realistic understanding of the "political" purpose of U.S. nukes in Europe is probably a combination of the idea that the U.S. military will fight for any nation in which it has stored nukes, the perverse prestige that many imagine comes with possessing nukes (even if someone else actually possesses them on your land), and the general U.S. goals of keeping European governments intertwined with the U.S. military, supportive of U.S. military strategies, and willing to spend vast amounts on U.S.-made weapons.

The presence of U.S. nuclear weapons is regularly protested by the public in the nations that host them.[17] In 1981, half a million people poured into the streets of Amsterdam to protest NATO's nuclear plans.[18] There were similar mass rallies in Rome, Bonn, and other Western European capitals. Popular opposition has put pressure on European governments. In 2019, the Belgian parliament almost passed a vote to remove nuclear weapons from Belgium.[19] Debate has raged among members of the German government and, in 2010, the German Parliament voted that the bombs should be removed from Germany, despite being forbidden to admit that they exist at all.[20] And yet the bombs remain. Europeans have also launched major campaigns to compel financial institutions to divest from nuclear weapons.[21]

Don't these weapons violate treaties to pursue nuclear disarmament?

Since 1970, the Treaty on the Non-Proliferation of Nuclear Weapons has required its nuclear-nation parties to "pursue negotiations in good faith on effective measures relating to cessation of the nuclear arms race at an early date and to nuclear disarmament, and on a treaty on general and complete disarmament under strict and effective international control." Parties to the treaty include the biggest five (Russia, United States, China, France, and Great Britain) but not the next four (Pakistan, India, Israel, and North Korea). Non-nuclear nations are also party to the treaty, including Germany, Italy, Belgium, the Netherlands, and Turkey.

Needless to say, the nuclear parties to the treaty are blatantly violating it by not pursuing nuclear disarmament, and by having developed cultural and societal worlds in which the very idea of general and complete disarmament sounds insane and nobody even bothers to mention that it is illegally being disregarded.

The same treaty also states that "Each nuclear-weapon State Party to the Treaty undertakes not to transfer to any recipient whatsoever nuclear weapons or other nuclear explosive devices or control over such weapons or explosive devices directly, or indirectly; and not in any way to assist, encourage, or induce any non-nuclear-weapon State to manufacture or otherwise acquire nuclear weapons or other nuclear explosive devices, or control over such weapons or explosive devices."

For the non-nuclear states, the flip side of this is also included: "Each non-nuclear-weapon State Party to the Treaty undertakes not to receive the transfer from any transferor whatsoever of nuclear weapons or other nuclear explosive devices or of control over such weapons or explosive devices directly, or indirectly; not to manufacture or otherwise acquire nuclear weapons or other nuclear explosive devices; and not to seek or receive any assistance in the manufacture of nuclear weapons or other nuclear explosive devices."

Yet the United States has transferred nuclear weapons to the territory of other nations, described them as NATO operations, and trained local pilots in nuclear bombing using the host country's airplanes. Does the fact that the United States keeps ownership of the nuclear weapons bring it into compliance with the law?

Since 2021, there has been a global effort to eliminate nuclear weapons through the Treaty on the Prohibition of

Nuclear Weapons. Signatories to this treaty have agreed that:

"Each State Party undertakes never under any circumstances to:

(a) Develop, test, produce, manufacture, otherwise acquire, possess or stockpile nuclear weapons or other nuclear explosive devices;

(b) Transfer to any recipient whatsoever nuclear weapons or other nuclear explosive devices or control over such weapons or explosive devices directly or indirectly;

(c) Receive the transfer of or control over nuclear weapons or other nuclear explosive devices directly or indirectly;

(d) Use or threaten to use nuclear weapons or other nuclear explosive devices;

(e) Assist, encourage or induce, in any way, anyone to engage in any activity prohibited to a State Party under this Treaty;

(f) Seek or receive any assistance, in any way, from anyone to engage in any activity prohibited to a State Party under this Treaty;

(g) Allow any stationing, installation or deployment of any nuclear weapons or other nuclear explosive devices in its territory or at any place under its jurisdiction or control."

As of this writing, 66 nations are party to the treaty, and popular movements are advancing it in many other nations. The current parties include five NATO partners: Ireland, Kazakhstan, Malta, Mongolia, and New Zealand. This is a potential problem for NATO's nuclear policy. As the world moves toward banning nuclear weapons, as banks that operate internationally divest from nuclear weapons, as corporations pull out of making nuclear weapons, the anti-nuclear agenda already has a foothold within NATO.

9

What Are the Divisions Within NATO?

Numerous issues have surfaced that have divided NATO members. Disagreements mostly flare up during the process of trying to achieve consensus on issues such as what new members to add, what wars to fight, and whom to make Secretary General.

In a 2020 report by NATO, in a section called "Strains on Allied Unity," NATO mentioned some of the divisions it has faced over the years: differences over the Vietnam war, dictatorships in its own ranks, the Euromissile debates, disagreements over enlargement, and the Iraq War.[1]

From the early years of NATO, France has been one of the most independent-minded members (or what a global policeman might call "insubordinate"). In 1966, under President Charles de Gaulle, France refused to integrate its nuclear weapons with other North Atlantic nations or to accept outside control over its armed forces. DeGaulle downgraded France's membership in NATO and withdrew France from the NATO Military Command Structure. But he also stated that France would remain in the alliance, and in 2009, France relented and rejoined the NATO Military Command Structure.

More recently, France was upset that it was cut out of submarine sales to Australia by the AUKUS weapons deal—er, we mean "security alliance."

Prior to the Russian invasion of Ukraine, France talked increasingly of the idea of a non-NATO European military. Since coming to power in 2017, French President Macron coined the term "European strategic autonomy." He envisioned a structure where the European nations would gain autonomy in decision-making, something the United States has repeatedly squashed. Macron even called NATO "brain-dead," drawing a backlash from other members. But Macron's criticism of NATO and talk about alternatives faded away with the Russian invasion of Ukraine.

Turkey has also been a frequent source of division within NATO. It has even less interest in democracy than some of the other NATO governments, and it has had a more independent foreign policy. In a December 2023 opinion column in *The Hill* newspaper in Washington, D.C., three U.S. think tank authors summarized:

"Turkey bought the S-400 (a Russian air defense system that threatens Washington's F-35 program), nearly upended NATO by threatening to invade Greece, almost hit U.S. troops in Syria, became the safe-haven for the Muslim Brotherhood after it was kicked out of Egypt, served as a financing arm for Hamas and Russia, and is engaging in a battle of threats with Israel over Ankara's support for Hamas. . . . Nonetheless, the U.S. continues extensive economic cooperation, delivery of humanitarian aid and agreeing to arms sales and security assistance that have been valued at nearly $478 billion since President Biden took office. . . . Turkey is once again evaluating whether it should approve of Sweden joining NATO. Now, in exchange for its vote, Turkey wants a simultaneous sale of the U.S.-produced advanced F-16 aircraft and drone cameras from Canada. . . . U.S. policymakers often operate under the assumption that sending more weapons to allies and strategic partners provides Washington leverage over the recipients. Yet, Turkey serves as the latest example that the opposite is true."[2]

Another concession to get Turkey's approval for Swedish membership was a crackdown on the Kurds living in Sweden. As *The Guardian* reported: "In an effort to win over [Turkish President Recep Tayyip] Erdoğan, say some, Swedish authorities are increasing surveillance of Kurdish people living in Sweden, subjecting asylum seekers to investigations by Säpo, the security police,

and closing down the bank accounts of Kurdish chari-
ties. There are also reports of dozens of innocent people's
residence permits being stopped. Last week, days after
Turkey approved Sweden's NATO application, it was
announced that public broadcaster Sveriges Radio would
be shutting its Kurdish newsroom."[3]

Even worse, perhaps, from NATO's perspective, has
been Turkey's peace initiatives. In 2003, Turkey refused
to allow the U.S. to use its territory for its illegal attack on
Iraq.[4] Turkey has maintained good relations with Russia
and hosted peace negotiations that almost ended the war
in Ukraine shortly after it began, and could still end it if
the United States goes along.

Despite all the contradictions, NATO members
would rather have Turkey on the inside than the outside,
so it remains in NATO and the discord continues.

Hungary under its authoritarian Prime Minister
Viktor Orban has also been a NATO outlier, maintaining good relations with Russia and creating obstacles
for sending weapons and financial aid to Ukraine. Along
with Turkey, Hungary also opposed the bid of Sweden to
join the alliance. Hungary was the last NATO member to
reach "consensus" on admitting Sweden, and did so once
Sweden agreed to sell Hungary some jet fighters.[5]

Of course, NATO remains very much divided, not
on whether to admit Ukraine, but when. And increasingly it is divided on the question of sending troops from

NATO countries into Ukraine, something proposed most prominently by French President Emmanuel Macron. Germany, Britain, Spain, Poland, and the Czech Republic immediately distanced themselves from Macron's remarks. "There will be no ground troops, no soldiers on Ukrainian soil sent there by European countries or NATO states," remarked German Chancellor Olaf Scholz.[6]

Ironically, perhaps the biggest strain in this "democratic alliance" has been over the reluctance of some NATO members to spend more on weapons. This is especially true in countries that have stronger democratic institutions, where people have fought hard to stop their governments from taking funds from their social welfare systems to dump into the black hole of militarism.

Is Donald Trump anti-NATO?

Dissent regarding NATO also emerged during Donald Trump's presidency, when he railed about NATO members not paying their fair share and called NATO obsolete. Congress was so jittery about Trump's criticism of NATO that it later passed legislation banning any president from exiting NATO.[7]

But reviewing Trump's performance as U.S. president from 2017 to 2021, we can surely conclude that, with enemies like Trump, NATO—and the global war machine—hardly needs friends.

Despite complaining that the U.S. was spending more than its "fair share," Trump increased U.S. military spending—just as Obama had done and Biden would do. He embraced his role as weapons-dealer-in-chief far more publicly than any other U.S. president, holding press conferences to brag about new weapons sales. He also allowed weapons shipments from the United States to Ukraine, something that President Barack Obama had refused to do out of fear that it could lead to war with Russia. Trump—widely reported as a friend or even a servant of the Russian government—also evicted Russian diplomats, sanctioned Russian officials, put missiles practically on Russia's border, lobbied European nations to drop Russian energy deals, left the Iran agreement, tore up the INF Treaty, rejected Russia's offers on banning weapons in space and banning cyberwar, expanded NATO eastward, added a NATO partner in Colombia, proposed adding Brazil, splurged on more nukes, bombed Russians in Syria, oversaw the largest war rehearsals in Europe in half a century (now outdone), condemned all proposals for a non-NATO European military, and insisted that Europe stick with NATO.

So, U.S. government support for NATO continues, no matter what political party is in power. Yes, potential for divisions abound and if they become too great, the United States may one day be tempted to abandon NATO, but only if it sees a superior path to dominating the globe.

As for the other NATO members, despite their periodic disagreements, in the end they fall in line. Remember, we are talking about a military alliance in which other militaries are generally subordinated to the U.S. military. Division is not allowed in a military.

10

What Are NATO's Plans?

NATO plans to grow, to add members, to add partners, to add bases, to add weapons, to add troops, and to engage more in the fields of policing, politics, academia, research, industry, and propaganda. NATO plans increased militarization and hostility toward Russia and China.[1]

Following years of buildup toward the war in Ukraine, during which many predicted that NATO expansion would lead to war, and some advocated for achieving just that result, the predicted war came and was immediately named "The Unprovoked War."[2]

In 2024 NATO members, such as Defense Minister of Germany Boris Pistorius, were warning that Russia will attack NATO within the next several years.[3] The Danish Defense Minister Troels Lund Poulse said three to five years.[4] The Chair of the NATO Military Committee, Admiral Rob Bauer of the Royal Netherlands Navy, urged escalated preparation for a NATO war with Russia. So did Sweden's commander-in-chief General Micael Bydén and Sweden's Minister for Civil Defense Carl-Oskar Bohlin, Poland's Defense Minister Władysław Kosiniak-Kamysz, and Lithuania's Foreign Minister Gabrielius Landsbergis.[5] Of course, all of these people, sincerely or otherwise, agreed that the only way to reduce the chance of war with Russia was to increase the very things that led to the war in Ukraine.

The inability or refusal to think in terms of negotiation and peaceful reconciliation with Russia has for years now also been preventing an end to the war in Ukraine. NATO members such as French President Emmanuel Macron have been talking up the idea of sending large numbers of Western troops into the war in Ukraine, thereby possibly speeding up by several years the arrival of an all-out NATO war with Russia.[6] NATO has not only added Sweden and Finland as members, but also added new missiles near Russia's border in Lithuania.[7] And—although our "free" and "democratic" governments did not tell us—we know from documents leaked in April 2023 that there were already at least 97 NATO "special forces" troops operating in Ukraine, including 50 British, 14 U.S., and 15 French.

Admiral John Kirby, the National Security Council spokesman, also acknowledged in April 2023 a "small U.S. military presence" based in the U.S. Embassy in Kyiv to try to keep track of thousands of tons of U.S. weapons as they arrive in Ukraine.[8] Many more U.S. forces, whether inside or outside Ukraine, have been involved in planning Ukrainian military operations;[9] providing satellite intelligence; and targeting of U.S.-made weapons.[10]

While not all NATO member nations are prepared to make Ukraine a NATO member, some, at NATO's urging, have signed or are working on signing their own bilateral, NATO-like agreements with Ukraine that include not only military support and interoperability but also a commitment to help Ukraine join NATO. These include the UK,[11] Estonia,[12] Greece,[13] France, Germany, Romania, Poland, and the Netherlands.[14]

Beyond a failure to make peace with Russia, many voices in NATO urge Russia's destruction. Kusti Salm, the permanent secretary at the Estonian Defense Ministry, advocates for "ruining" Russia.[15] Former Raytheon Board Member and current U.S. Secretary of Defense Lloyd Austin has said that the U.S. goal in Ukraine is to weaken Russia.[16] U.S. Senator Lindsey Graham has publicly urged the assassination of Russian President Vladimir Putin.[17] Communications between the U.S./NATO and Russian militaries have been cut off at the same time that no buffer remains (as during the previous Cold War) between NATO and Russia, almost no disarmament treaties remain, and NATO claims to "intercept" hundreds of Russian military airplanes annually.[18] A NATO map and list of its weapons and troops on the Russian border is staggering. It could be a history textbook illustration for the section on World War III, were people and textbooks likely to exist following World War III.[19]

As we write, NATO is engaging 90,000 troops in the largest war rehearsal since the previous Cold War.[20] The German military has drawn up its own plans for how a major NATO-Russia war could be begun by each side building up more troops and weapons and fears near their border—exactly what NATO is in fact pursuing.[21] NATO's war rehearsals include the cyber variety as well.[22]

Nations NATO loves to hate

NATO's hostility toward Russia, and toward China as well, only encourages the worst militarist tendencies in those countries, and only moves them closer to each other, giving NATO reasons to oppose them both all the more.

In the U.S. Congress in recent years, possibly the leading topic of discussion has been China, competition with China, fear of China, hostility toward China. The need for economic competition with China is simply assumed without argument, and any line between economic competition and military antagonism is generally avoided.

But U.S. antagonism toward China has created a dilemma for many European countries that are dependent on China for trade. Although the U.S. trades more with China than with nearly any other country, the European allies are more exposed because their economies are more trade dependent. According to the International Monetary Fund, the rupture of investment between the West and China would lower European GDP by 2%, more than twice that of the U.S.[23] Even worse would be a U.S. war with China over Taiwan, which NATO members would be reluctant to support.

That is why, in 2019, U.S. pressure on NATO allies to adopt a more aggressive posture toward China provoked an indignant response from French President Macron. "Is our enemy today Russia? Or China?" he asked rhetorically. "Is it the goal of NATO to designate them as enemies? I don't think so."

But the very next year, European allies fell in line and antagonism toward China became official NATO policy.

In the words of a 2020 NATO report,

"NATO must devote much more time, political resources, and action to the security challenges posed by China—based on an assessment of its national capabilities, economic heft, and the stated ideological goals of its leaders. It needs to develop a political strategy for approaching a world in which China will be of growing importance through to 2030. The Alliance should infuse the China challenge throughout existing structures and consider establishing a consultative body to discuss all aspects of Allies' security interests vis-à-vis China. It must expand efforts to assess the implications of China's technological development and monitor and defend against any Chinese activities that could impact collective defence, military readiness or resilience in the Supreme Allied Commander Europe's (SACEUR) Area of Responsibility."[24]

NATO's 2022 Strategic Concept was even more aggressive, claiming that "China's stated ambitions and coercive policies challenge our interests, security and values. Allies will work together to address the systemic challenges posed by China to Euro-Atlantic security."

NATO supporters insist that flashpoints like Taiwan, South China Sea, East China Sea, and the China-India boundary dispute must be part of the Alliance's future-oriented security strategy. This is why NATO is strengthening its relationships in the Indo-Pacific.

As NATO tentacles reach into the Indo-Pacific, NATO is also seeking a greater presence across the Global South, including in Western Asia and North Africa, areas that NATO calls its "southern neighborhood" in a disturbing parallel to U.S. references to Latin America as its backyard.[25] In the Arctic, NATO seeks to control waters that are opening up as the ice melts, in particular to control access to more fossil fuels with which to cause more of the ice to melt. At the same time, NATO is putting ever more effort into pretending to be a "green" operation.

As if this global reach were not enough, U.S. politicians, including Donald Trump, have been scolding NATO for not being more involved in counterterrorism. NATO is trying to rectify that. As it said in its "NATO 2030: United For a New Era" concept paper:

"Terrorism poses one of the most immediate, asymmetric threats to Allied nations and citizens. NATO should more explicitly integrate the fight against terrorism into its core tasks. This fight should be given a place within NATO structures, supported by necessary resources, commensurate with the threat that it poses. NATO should enhance the fight against terrorism as part of the hybrid and cyber conversation and ensure that the threat from terrorism figures in exercises and lessons learned. NATO should strive to improve current practices of intelligence-sharing among Allies to achieve better, common situational awareness in key areas including emerging safe havens and terrorists' use of EDTs [emerging and disruptive technologies], as well as hybrid tactics."[26]

And let's not forget that NATO's many-tentacled future ambitions include joint high-tech research, where it envisions the following:

"NATO should consider developing a North Atlantic equivalent of the U.S. Defence Advanced Research Projects Agency (DARPA) or European Defence Fund (EDF) charged with encouraging support for innovation in strategic areas among Allies. Such an entity could be supported by an Advisory Group for Small and Medium Enterprises (SME) to the NATO Industrial Advisory Group (NIAG) to advise the Alliance on how to keep pace with technological change. A key objective for these efforts should be to encourage the development of an AI-focused agenda for R&D within the Alliance."[27]

What could go wrong?

11

What Are the Alternatives?

Supporters of Russia claim that Russia had to invade Ukraine to push back against NATO expansion, even though it was perfectly predictable that the invasion would give NATO an enormous boost.

Supporters of NATO claim that the only possible response to Russian warmaking is more NATO expansion, knowing perfectly well that nothing will better encourage Russian militarism.

So, we are getting more NATO bases in Finland, and more Russian troops near Finland, and yet more NATO bases in Finland. We are getting more U.S. nukes in Europe, and more Russian nukes in Europe. Arms races and threats are vicious cycles that increase the risk of nuclear war, already now the greatest it has ever been, according to numerous observers and the Doomsday Clock.[1] The militarization is exacerbated by propaganda. Phrases like "with Putin now openly threatening Europe's borders" show up in Western media without any link or reference to Putin threatening Europe's borders.[2]

There are always alternatives. It is hard to think of an alternative to 20 years of war in Afghanistan that would have been worse than what was done. Simply not doing it would have been an infinitely better alternative. Peace negotiations in Libya and Ukraine were blocked by NATO, which opted for war. An obvious alternative would have been to negotiate peace—or, in the case of Ukraine—to simply abide by existing agreements like those made in the 2015 Minsk Accords.

The idea that any war could not possibly have been prevented due to the other side's intransigence is nonsense that obfuscates the potential to be found in all variety of diplomacy and nonviolent action. With any particular war, there are always clear steps that could have been taken to avoid it.

What about neutrality?

A nation is not required by any laws of physics to be loyal to NATO or an enemy of NATO. It can be neutral. During the Cold War, there were states in Europe that were neither part of NATO nor the Warsaw Pact. They were either neutral or members of the global Non-Aligned Movement. The neutral countries were Austria, Switzerland, Ireland, Finland, and Sweden, until Finland and

Sweden joined NATO in the wake of Russia's invasion of Ukraine. The Non-Aligned Countries were Yugoslavia, Cyprus, and Malta. All of them shared a determination to remain independent and to advocate for peace and disarmament.

Neutral states are not supposed to allow *any* foreign military within their territory, but Ireland has a long history of allowing military aircraft of various nations to refuel at Shannon Airport—an option that the United States used regularly in the wake of the 9/11 attacks. Unlike other neutral states, Irish governments have said that allowing aircraft to use Irish soil does not constitute participation in any particular conflict and is compatible with a neutral stance.

Whether or not a nation is officially a neutral one, it can choose to be neutral on particular wars. Most nations are neutral on most wars. When the U.S. government tried to force nations to side with it on the war in Ukraine, much of the world refused to do so. Neutrality is easier when a war is distant and disconnected. But we need neutrality to be applied universally—neutrality on all wars, near and far.

Nations not ready to follow the wisdom of Costa Rica and abolish their militaries, and governments too afraid of their own people to train them in unarmed civilian resistance, can still commit to only fighting defensive wars. And though preparation for defensive wars tends to lead to wars and also to the militarization of domestic society—and though indigenous groups have defended their land without war, and peoples have overthrown dictators without war—commiting to only fight defensive wars could still mean a huge step in the right direction.

The choice facing many countries is not neutrality or militarization, but neutrality or incorporation into a foreign empire and its global war machine, neutrality or subservience to a global Monroe Doctrine.

South Africa and Nicaragua took steps in 2024 to uphold the rule of law in Palestine through the International Court of Justice. They took steps that neutral countries could also have taken. They did not send weapons to Palestinians. They did not support a vicious cycle of war madness. They proposed that the Israeli government be stopped from committing genocide by holding it accountable to international law. Only a government with some degree of neutrality could have done that. Arguably, many governments failed to do the same precisely because they are not neutral.

The nations professing or engaging in neutrality of one sort or another are losing Sweden and Finland, as a result of the catastrophe in Ukraine that neutrality could have prevented and that probably cannot be ended without some sort of neutrality. Sweden and Finland may come to regret their choice. When you join a military alliance, you become a possible target for its enemies, sometimes even a more likely target than the home capital of the empire. Ukraine is being treated as a sacrifice zone, and Finland should expect nothing else.

Can't we just abolish war?

Were there a war that did more good than harm, as is imagined in "just war theory," that unusual war would still never do enough good to outweigh having kept the institution of war, the standing armies, the bases, the ships, and the planes around waiting for the "just war" to arrive. Military preparedness actually generates wars, most of which nobody tries to defend as just.

And war takes a toll much greater than its human victims. War causes environmental destruction, promotes bigotry, erodes the rule of law, provides justification for secrecy in governance, and, most of all, diverts resources from human needs.

There are numerous sufficient reasons to abolish war. It is immoral, it endangers lives, it erodes liberty, it promotes bigotry, it wastes $2 trillion a year, it threatens the environment, it impoverishes us, and alternatives do exist. So, the bad news is that war ruins everything it touches and it touches darn near everything. The good news is that, if we could see past the flags and propaganda, we could build a massive coalition of nearly everyone—including even most of the people making the weapons, who would be happier and better off with other jobs. We could create, for far less than is spent on wars, investment in climate protection, and eliminate homelessness, poverty, and disease. A nation that aided others in those ways would, incidentally, make itself safer than any military ever could.[3]

Can unarmed resistance make a difference?

There are countless examples of successful nonviolent resistance to war. Some are well known, such as Gandhi's nonviolent actions to remove the British from India, others forgotten. In Lebanon, 30 years of Syrian domination was ended through a large-scale, nonviolent uprising in 2005. In Algeria in 1961, four French generals staged a coup; nonviolent resistance undid it in a few days. In the First Intifada in the 1980s, much of the subjugated Palestinian population effectively became self-governing entities through nonviolent non-cooperation. Nonviolent movements have removed U.S. bases from Ecuador and the Philippines.

In the Soviet Union in 1991, the late Mikhail Gorbachev was arrested, tanks sent into major cities, media shut down, and protests banned; nonviolent protests ended the coup in a few days. Lithuania, Latvia, and Estonia freed themselves from Soviet occupation through nonviolent resistance prior to the USSR's collapse, and not through military action by NATO or anyone else. Everyone should watch a film about Estonia called *The Singing Revolution*. You would not believe us if we described it.

When the Soviet military invaded Czechoslovakia in 1968, there were demonstrations, a general strike, refusal to cooperate, removal of street signs, persuasion of troops. Despite clueless leaders conceding, the take-over was slowed, and the credibility of the Soviet Communist Party ruined.[4]

When Russia invaded Ukraine, there were hundreds of incidents of Ukrainians using unarmed resistance, despite their government's choice of armed fighting. Nonviolent actions in Ukraine blocked tanks, talked soldiers out of fighting, and pushed soldiers out of entire neighborhoods. Unarmed civilians kept the Russian military away from the Zaporizhzhia nuclear plant, without a single death, whereas handing that job over to the National Guard resulted in an immediate takeover by the Russians, who dangerously fired on the nuclear plant once there were armed troops there to fire on.

It is a high hurdle to create an unarmed civil defense plan once a country has been militarily invaded, especially after decades of military preparations and the accompanying cultural indoctrination in the supposed necessity of military defense. That is why governments that are not at war should learn about and establish departments of unarmed civilian defense. A properly prepared unarmed defense department (something that might require an investment of a mere 2 or 3% of a military budget) could make a nation ungovernable if attacked by another country.

Nations without militaries, such as Costa Rica and Iceland, could develop robust unarmed defense departments. But nations with militaries, and with militaries and weapons industries subservient to imperial powers, will have the harder task of developing unarmed defense. This task will be much easier, however, as long as such nations are not at war. It would be made even easier by developing governments that truly represented the will of their people. An unrepresentative government will fear the creation of unarmed civilian defense, not because it is not a powerful tool for deterring and protecting against foreign attack, but because it is also a powerful tool for opposing misgovernment from within.

What could the U.S. government do instead of supporting NATO?

Instead of supporting NATO and military interventions worldwide, the U.S. could—and should—join international treaties to foster peace. These include:

- The Landmines Treaty,
- The Arms Trade Treaty,
- The Convention on Cluster Munitions,
- The Treaty on the Prohibition of Nuclear Weapons,
- The International Criminal Court.

What else could the U.S. do? It could end the practice of punishing other nations for supporting international courts. It could begin nuclear disarmament, and negotiations with other nuclear nations to disarm in compliance with the Treaty on Non-Proliferation that it has signed but not implemented. It could support the negotiation of treaties on weapons in space and on cyberwars. It could close the hundreds of military bases outside the United States. It could end the practice of sanctioning whole nations.

This, of course, would be a radically different approach to the world that would require a radical reorientation of priorities. But when the status quo is making nuclear apocalypse increasingly likely and robbing the resources needed to address real problems like climate change, a radical shift is essential. NATO is not a tenable option. In fact, when we hear the acronym NATO, that is what we should think of: Not A Tenable Option.

What does the non-NATO world think of the military alliance?

A December 2014 Gallup poll of global public opinion across 65 nations found the United States to be, by far, the country considered the largest threat to peace in the world.[5] The findings were made public and the lesson learned: Gallup never did that poll again.

A Pew poll in 30 countries in 2017 found majorities in most countries polled viewing the United States' "power and influence" as a threat. In Russia 79% viewed the U.S. as a major or a minor threat; in Mexico that figure was 85%, in Japan 84%, in Turkey 87%, in Germany 80%, in France 79%, in Spain 79%, in Australia 76%, in the UK 74%, in Canada 74%, in the Netherlands 74%, etc. The numbers are staggering. The numbers for those who viewed China and Russia as threats were also significant, but smaller than for the United States.[6]

In 2017, former NATO Secretary General and former Danish Prime Minister Anders Fogh Rasmussen co-founded an organization called the Alliance of Democracies Foundation. This foundation claimed that the United States was irresponsibly retreating from the world and allowing a vacuum to be filled by autocrats or dictators (not the ones the U.S. arms and trains, but just the designated enemies of NATO: Vladimir Putin, Kim Jong-un, and Bashar al-Assad).

In 2021, the Alliance of Democracies Foundation made the mistake of polling 50,000 respondents in 53 countries. The poll found that 44% of respondents were concerned that the United States threatened democracy in their country. The same number for those concerned about a threat from China was 38% and Russia 28%. This, of course, means that NATO and former NATO bigwigs are claiming to defend democracy from places that are viewed as less of a threat to democracy than is the dominant member of NATO.[7]

In 2024 the Arab Center Washington DC surveyed 8,000 individuals across 16 countries in the Arab world. When asked about the countries that most threatened the security and stability of the Arab region, 51% of respondents said that the policies of the United States were the most threatening.[8]

There do not seem to be a lot of public global polls of non-NATO countries on the topic of NATO. If people view NATO as a moderating force on the United States, or if they have no idea what NATO is, then NATO might fare better than did the United States in the polls above. But if NATO is understood as a vehicle for strengthening the power of the U.S. military and of U.S. influence, then it might fare even worse.

There is one poll from 2022 by Gallup. Gallup did not poll in Russia or China. Support for NATO was at a whopping 5% in Serbia, 7% in Yemen, 8% in Iran, 9% in

Pakistan, 9% in Afghanistan, 11% in Ethiopia, 11% in Libya, 15% in Morocco, 17% in Indonesia, 20% in NATO member Turkey, and 21% in Greece. In the entire continent of Africa, only in Kenya (53%) and Liberia (58%) did support for NATO exceed 50%. Nowhere in Latin America did it rise above 35%. In Asia it topped 50% only in New Zealand and Australia.

Here is how Gallup reported this:

"Gallup's first global measure of perceptions of the organization's leadership in 2022 showed that across 138 countries, median global approval of NATO's leadership stood at 34%. Slightly fewer worldwide disapproved (30%) of the alliance, but a high percentage (27%) also did not have an opinion—which speaks to NATO's relatively limited visibility outside of its membership. Among NATO member countries, median approval of the alliance's leadership in 2022 stood at a robust 64%. In contrast, approval was half as high among non-member nations, with median approval sitting at 31% among non-member states and just as many disapproving (31%) or lacking an opinion (31%)."[9]

It seems that, in NATO countries, NATO is not seen as the same sort of threat as the United States is; however, in non-NATO countries, it is seen as an even greater one. So, within the NATO world, NATO is a good front for the U.S. military. A NATO press conference is going to play better than a Pentagon one. But in the rest of the world, it is better to keep quiet about NATO during the quest to "win hearts and minds."

Where polling and public debate are more robust is in nations considering joining NATO. There is a big popular pushback right now in Ireland against the idea of joining NATO and losing Ireland's neutrality.[10] One organization advocating strongly for neutrality is the Peace and Neutrality Alliance (PANA). In nations further to the east (Ukraine, Sweden, Finland), strong majorities opposed joining NATO for years, but the Russian invasion of Ukraine changed all that, sending support for NATO membership through the roof.[11]

Polling by the U.S.-government-funded International Republican Institute showed that, between 2021 and 2023, support for NATO membership climbed from 21% to 26% in Moldova, 77% to 80% in Georgia, 54% to 82% in Ukraine, and 89% to 95% in Kosovo.[12]

Is there much popular opposition in NATO countries?

Polling within most NATO countries finds majority support for NATO—if not necessarily for any particular thing it does.[13] Opinion against, and activism against, particular wars is highest, followed by opinion and activism against the spending of particular mountains of money, followed—bringing up the rear—by opinion and activism against NATO itself.

A February 2024 Gallup poll looking at NATO support in the U.S. found that 47% of Americans wanted to see the United States keep its current level of commitment, 20% wanted to increase it, and 28% wanted to either decrease it or withdraw entirely.[14]

There was a major gap between Democrats and Republicans, though, with only 14% of Democrats wanting less or no participation vs 42% of Republicans. One reason is that some Republicans lean toward isolationism and believe Europe should take care of its own problems. Another reason is that Donald Trump is widely reported as opposing NATO, although he has actually been far more interested in getting NATO members to buy more U.S. weapons.

There is, however, a good deal of activism in the United States and throughout the NATO world, in favor of scaling back and abolishing NATO, not because some of its members do not buy enough weapons, but because it promotes militarism, war, the risk of nuclear holocaust, environmental destruction, international hostility, and lawlessness. These opponents of NATO express a preference for a world of cooperation, disarmament, and investment in human and environmental needs.

Within NATO nations, it is easier to build coalitions and movements against particular wars or weapons than against warmaking as a whole, and easier to oppose warmaking as a whole than to oppose NATO, which is seen by some as almost a legitimizer of just and proper wars by "the international community."

In recent years, new NATO member Montenegro, at the direction of NATO and the United States, sought to build an enormous military training ground, far too large for the entire military of Montenegro, to be used by NATO forces. Local residents put their bodies on the line as human shields to prevent it. They organized events, handed in petitions, put up billboards, met with government officials, marched, protested, and—as of this moment—seem to have finally succeeded in eliminating the plans to destroy their mountain plateau for NATO.[15]

So NATO can be stopped by popular movements. But it should be noted that the case made by activists in Montenegro was not so much against NATO because of what it does to the world, as against local environmental and cultural destruction no matter who was going to do it, no matter for how noble a cause.

In Germany, the Netherlands, Belgium, Italy, the UK, and elsewhere in Europe, there is a fair amount of activism against NATO and U.S. bases, and in particular against the storing of nuclear weapons. Nonviolent protesters have repeatedly risked arrest and prison to oppose nuclear weapons.[16] Huge marches oppose the use of bases for drone wars.

In Chicago in 2012, a big march and rally protested a NATO summit (although Amnesty International put up advertisements thanking NATO for its war in Afghanistan).[17] In 2019 in Washington, D.C., World BEYOND War and CODEPINK held a conference and festival to protest a NATO meeting.[18]

An international coalition was formed in 2009 (see no-to-nato.org) that includes 650 organizations in more than 30 countries. The coalition has protested NATO meetings throughout Europe year after year, and promoted alternatives to NATO widely.

In 2023 a group was formed under the name Global Women for Peace United Against NATO. It has been putting out material educating the public about NATO. (See womenagainstnato.org.)

Beginning in 2022, the International Peace Bureau and World BEYOND War have been organizing an annual 24-hour live-Zoomed "peace wave" with video of events opposing NATO and making the case for peace. (See 24hourpeacewave.org.)

Peace groups in Belgium, where NATO is headquartered, have played a major role in opposing NATO. (See vrede.be.)

In the UK, peace groups have shown strong opposition to NATO. (See no2nato.org.)

April 4th is NATO's yearly celebration of its own creation, and those who oppose it advocate for a different path, as well as—especially in the United States—marking the date of Dr. Martin Luther King, Jr.'s speech against war at Riverside Church, one year before his assassination.

For NATO's 75th Anniversary meetings in Washington, D.C., in July 2024, a coalition of organizations organized a counter-summit and a protest rally in front of the White House. (See nonatoyespeace.org.) These include the Campaign for Nuclear Disarmament, CODEPINK, DSA International Committee, Global Network Against Weapons & Nuclear Power in Space, Global Women for Peace United Against NATO, International Peace Bureau, NC Peace Action, No to War – No to NATO, Nuclear Age Peace Foundation, RootsAction.org, United National Antiwar Coalition, Veterans For Peace, Vrede, Women's International League for Peace and Freedom US, and World BEYOND War.

They put out this short statement:

"The North Atlantic Treaty Organization is a destabilizing, law-breaking force for militarization and war provocation. Its existence makes wars, including nuclear wars, more likely. Its hostility toward the few significant militaries in the world that are not among its members fuels arms races and conflicts. The commitment of NATO members to join each others' wars and NATO's pursuit of enemies far from the North Atlantic risk global destruction.

We hold up a vision of a world beyond NATO, where we invest to eliminate poverty, hunger, illness and homelessness; where we live in harmony with our environment; and where we resolve conflict diplomatically through the only global organization that represents the whole world—the United Nations."

Here in the United States, we have seen, even in recent years, how public pressure from the U.S. and global public has prevented war. From the Obama administration to the Biden administration, forces in the U.S. have pushed for a war with Iran; public opposition has played a key role in preventing that. During the Obama presidency, public resistance in Europe and the United States prevented a massive escalation of a war on Syria. Public opposition did not stop the United States from attacking Iraq in 2003, but did stop NATO from supporting it.

With the horrific genocide in Gaza that followed the October 7, 2023, Hamas attack on Israel, public opposition exploded throughout the world and forced governments that were long-time supporters of Israel to change policy.

In the U.S. and around the world, we must build global opposition not just to individual conflicts, but to all wars. And right now, the supreme war-making alliance is NATO. While NATO is basking in the unity that followed Russia's war in Ukraine, that unity will be short-lived. We are already seeing the cracks, with some countries urging peace talks while others call for "victory."

If we are to prevent another devastating global conflict and move toward a world that is not based on military alliances but on win-win, peaceful cooperation among nations, our task is clear: We must build a global grassroots movement to Say No to NATO and No to War.

Acknowledgements

We would like to thank our organizations. For CODEPINK, Medea would like to thank her dear co-founder Jodie Evans, the wonderful co-directors Farida Alam and Danaka Katovich, as well as the terrific staff and volunteers around the country who inspire us with their commitment and creative activism to end war. David would like to thank World BEYOND War, its wonderful board, staff, advisory board, and volunteer heroes for peace, as well as the tremendous staff of RootsAction.org.

We are immensely grateful to Nicolas J. S. Davis for his help in writing and editing, especially the sections on NATO's wars. It is always such a pleasure to work with you. The same for our meticulous editor Bill Montross, who volunteers at a moment's notice and somehow catches every darn mistake we make.

We want to acknowledge the No to NATO Campaign which, for 15 years has been keeping us focused on the NATO problem. We are grateful to our publisher, Colin Robinson of OR Books, who agreed to take this book on in record time for NATO's 75th anniversary, understanding the importance of getting this information out to a public that knows very little about the inner workings of this military alliance run amok.

Finally, we want to thank our families. Medea would like to thank her partner Tighe Barry for his love, his encouragement and for putting up with her never-ending and very time-consuming projects to confront the war machine. David wants to thank his parents, his wife Anna, Anna's parents, his sister, and her family, and his two amazing sons.

Notes

Introduction

1   *The Economist*, "Emmanuel Macron Warns Europe: NATO Is Becoming Brain Dead," November 7, 2019, https://www.economist.com/europe/2019/11/07/emmanuel-macron-warns-europe-nato-is-becoming-brain-dead.

2   Ashley Parker, "Donald Trump Says NATO Is 'Obsolete,'" *The New York Times*, April 2, 2016, https://archive.nytimes.com/www.nytimes.com/politics/first-draft/2016/04/02/donald-trump-tells-crowd-hed-be-fine-if-nato-broke-up.

3   Par Frédéric Mauro, "NATO Is dead but Europe Is sick," IRIS, November 21, 2019, https://www.iris-france.org/142449-nato-is-dead-but-europe-is-sick.

4   U.S. Senate Foreign Relations Committee, "Cardin, Risch, Shaheen, Ricketts Introduce Resolution Recognizing NATO's 75th Anniversary," April 10, 2024, https://www.foreign.senate.gov/press/dem/release/cardin-risch-shaheen-ricketts-introduce-resolution-recognizing-natos-75th-anniversary.

1: When And Why Was NATO Formed?

1   Teri Schultz, "NATO celebrates 75 years with a new sense
    of purpose and an old threat," NPR, April 4, 2024, https://
    www.npr.org/2024/04/04/1242933676/nato-celebrates-
    75-years-with-a-new-sense-of-purpose-and-an-old-threat.

2   NATO, "The North Atlantic Treaty," NATO.int, April 4, 1949,
    https://www.nato.int/cps/en/natolive/official_texts_17120.htm.

3   NATO, "Collective Defense and Article 5," NATO.int, July 4,
    2023, https://www.nato.int/cps/en/natohq/topics_110496.
    htm.

4   Pawel Wargan, "NATO and the Long War on the Third
    World," *Monthly Review*, January 1, 2023, https://
    monthlyreview.org/2023/01/01/nato-and-the-long-war-
    on-the-third-world.

5   NATO, "France and NATO," NATO.int, https://www.nato.
    int/cps/en/natohq/declassified_160672.htm (accessed
    April 11, 2024).

6   Jawaharlal Nehru, "World Peace and Cooperation,"
    Universidad de la Laguna, April 22, 1955, https://pdcrodas.
    webs.ull.es/anglo/NehruWorldPeaceAndCooperation.pdf.

7   Wargan, "NATO and the Long War."

8   Thomas L. Hughes, "The Significance of NATO Present
    and Future," National Security Archive, August 13, 1965,
    https://nsarchive.gwu.edu/document/17558-document-13-
    inr-thomas-l-hughes-secretary.

9   C.H. Donnelly, "The Strategic Concept for the Defense
    of the North Atlantic Area," NATO.int, December 1, 1949,
    https://www.nato.int/docu/stratdoc/eng/a491201a.pdf.

10 Joseph R. Biden, "Speech Before the Euro-Atlantic Association in Warsaw," U.S. Embassy and Consulate in Poland, March 25, 1997, https://pl.usembassy.gov/senator_biden_speech.

11 Benjamin Schwarz, "'Cold War' Continuities: US Economic and Security Strategy Towards Europe," Benjaminschwarz.org, December 1, 1994, https://benjaminschwarz.org/1994/12/01/cold-war-continuities-us-economic-and-security-strategy-towards-europe.

12 Ibid.

13 NATO, "What Was the Warsaw Pact?" NATO.int, https://www.nato.int/cps/en/natohq/declassified_138294.htm (accessed April 11, 2024).

14 "The Warsaw Pact," San Diego State University, May 1, 1955, https://loveman.sdsu.edu/docs/1955Warsaw_Pact.pdf.

2: Nato Expansion

1 NATO, "The North Atlantic Treaty."

2 NATO, "NATO Enlargement & Open Door," NATO. int, https://www.nato.int/nato_static_fl2014/assets/pdf/pdf_2016_07/20160627_1607-factsheet-enlargement-eng.pdf (accessed April 11, 2024).

3 Ivan Gabal, "The Impact of NATO Membership in the Czech Republic, March 2022, https://www.files.ethz.ch/isn/97457/02_Mar_2.pdf.

4 National Security Archive, "NATO Expansion: What Gorbachev Heard," National Security Archive, December

12, 2017, https://nsarchive.gwu.edu/briefing-book/russia-programs/2017-12-12/nato-expansion-what-gorbachev-heard-western-leaders-early.

5   William Noah Glucroft, "NATO: Why Russia has a problem with its eastward expansion," Deutsche Welle, February 23, 2022, https://www.dw.com/en/nato-why-russia-has-a-problem-with-its-eastward-expansion/a-60891681.

6   Stan Resor, "Opposition to NATO Expansion," Arms Control Association, June 26, 1997, https://www.armscontrol.org/act/1997-06/arms-control-today/opposition-nato-expansion.

7   Ted Galen Carpenter, "Many Predicted NATO Expansion Would Lead to War. Those Warnings Were Ignored," The Guardian, February 28, 2022, https://www.theguardian.com/commentisfree/2022/feb/28/nato-expansion-war-russia-ukraine.

8   George F. Kennan, "A Fateful Error," *The New York Times*, February 5, 1997, https://www.nytimes.com/1997/02/05/opinion/a-fateful-error.html.

9   Ibid.

10 Congressional Record Volume 168, Number 27, Pages S632–S636, February 10, 2022, https://www.govinfo.gov/content/pkg/CREC-2022-02-10/html/CREC-2022-02-10-pt1-PgS632-2.htm.

11 Vladimir Putin, "A Speech Delivered at the MSC 2007," Masarykovy University, https://is.muni.cz/th/xlghl/DP_Fillinger_Speeches.pdf (accessed April 12, 2024).

12   Sarakshi Rai, "How Does a Country Become Part of
      NATO?" The Hill, May 19, 2022, https://thehill.com/policy/
      international/3494436-how-does-a-country-become-part-
      of-nato.

13   Lucia Mackenzie, "What Sweden brings to NATO,"
      Politico, March 7, 2024, https://www.politico.eu/article/
      sweden-nato-membership-military-power.

14   Tim Martin, " Saab Predicts 'great possibilities' in
      Sweden's NATO entry, warns of supplier 'ecosystem'
      issues," Breaking Defense, April 26, 2023, https://
      breakingdefense.com/2023/04/saab-predicts-great-
      possibilities-in-swedens-nato-entry-warns-of-supplier-
      ecosystem-issues.

15   Finnish Institute of International Affairs, "Finland in
      Afghanistan 2001–2021: From stabilization to advancing
      foreign and security policy relations,"
      Finnish Institute of International Affairs, December
      19, 2022, https://www.fiia.fi/en/publication/finland-in-
      afghanistan-2001-2021.

3: NATO's History of Aggression

1   United Nations, "United Nations Charter," United Nations,
      https://www.un.org/en/about-us/un-charter/full-text
      (accessed April 12, 2024).

2   Frontline, "Kosovo Facts and Figures," PBS, https://www.
      pbs.org/wgbh/pages/frontline/shows/kosovo/etc/facts.
      html (accessed April 12, 2024).

3   Ian Traynor, "Former war crimes prosecutor alleges
    Kosovan army harvested organs from Serb prisoners," The
    Guardian, April 11, 2008, https://www.theguardian.com/
    world/2008/apr/12/warcrimes.kosovo.

4   Balkan Insight, "Council Adopts Kosovo Organ Trafficking
    Resolution," Balkan Insight, January 25, 2011, https://
    balkaninsight.com/2011/01/25/council-adopts-kosovo-
    organ-trafficking-resolution.

5   Tom Walker and Aidan Laverty, "CIA Aided Kosovo
    Guerrilla Army All Along," Sunday Times (London) via
    Global Policy Forum, March 12, 2000, https://archive.
    globalpolicy.org/component/content/article/192-
    kosovo/38782.html.

6   John Flaherty and Jared Israel, "William Walker (Alias Mr.
    Racak) and His Salvador Massacre Coverup," 60 Minutes
    via Emperor's Clothes, March 22, 2002, http://emperors-
    clothes.com/analysis/sixty.htm.

7   Politika, Tanjug, "Controversy over events that triggered
    NATO attacks," WayBackMachine, October 22, 2008,
    https://web.archive.org/web/20081022225255/
    http:/www.b92.net/eng/news/politics-article.
    php?yyyy=2008&mm=10&dd=22&nav_id=54412.

8   J. Rainio, K. Lalu, and A. Penttilä, "Independent
    forensic autopsies in an armed conflict: investigation
    of the victims from Racak, Kosovo," Forensic Science
    International, February 13, 2001, http://balkanwitness.
    glypx.com/racakautopsies.htm.

9   Christophe Châtelet, "Kosovo: les morts de Racak ont-
    ils vraiment été massacrés froidement?," Le Monde,

January 21, 1999, https://www.lemonde.fr/archives/article/1999/01/21/les-morts-de-racak-ont-ils-vraiment-ete-massacres-froidement_3533047_1819218.html.

10 The Guardian, "Recak bodies 'were tampered with'," The Guardian, January 21, 1999, https://www.theguardian.com/world/1999/jan/21/8.

11 "Appendix B from the Interim Agreement for Peace and Self-Government In Kosovo," Serendipity, February 23, 1999, https://www.serendipity.li/nato/app_b.htm.

12 James Carafano and Janice Smith, "The Muddled Notion of Human Security at the U.N.: A Guide for U.S. Policymakers," The Heritage Foundation, September 1, 2006, https://www.heritage.org/report/the-muddled-notion-human-security-the-un-guide-forus-policymakers.

13 Diana Johnstone, Fools' Crusade: Yugoslavia, NATO and Western Delusions (Yugoslavia, NATO and Western Illusions), Pluto Press; 1st edition (September 20, 2002).

14 *Frontline*, "Kosovo Facts."

15 The Guardian, "Truth behind America's raid on Belgrade," *The Guardian*, November 27, 1999, https://www.theguardian.com/theobserver/1999/nov/28/focus.news1.

16 "Declaration by the Government of Cuba," June 1, 1999, http://www.cuba.cu/gobierno/documentos/1999/ing/d010699i.html.

17 Wikipedia, "Incident at Pristina airport," Wikipedia, https://en.wikipedia.org/wiki/Incident_at_Pristina_airport (accessed April 12, 2024).

18 Deutsche Welle, "Questions Arise Over US Base in Kosovo," Deutsche Welle, December 10, 2005,

https://www.dw.com/en/questions-arise-over-us-base-in-kosovo/a-1810615.

19   The Guardian, "Nato bombing 'caused ethnic cleansing' says Carrington," The Guardian, August 27, 1999, https://www.theguardian.com/world/1999/aug/27/balkans.

20   Diana Johnstone, "NATO's Kosovo Colony," Counterpunch via Third World Traveler, February 18, 2008, https://thirdworldtraveler.com/Europe/Kosovo_NATO_Colony.html.

21   Peter Klebnikov, "Heroin Heroes," Mother Jones, February 2000, https://books.google.com/books?id=mOcDAAAAMBAJ&pg=PA64#v=onepage&q&f=false.

22   Ian Traynor, "Nato force 'feeds Kosovo sex trade'," *The Guardian*, May 6, 2004, https://www.theguardian.com/world/2004/may/07/balkans.

23   Wikipedia, "List of sovereign states in Europe by GDP (nominal) per capita," Wikipedia, https://en.wikipedia.org/wiki/List_of_sovereign_states_in_Europe_by_GDP_(nominal)_per_capita (accessed April 12, 2004).

24   Medea Benjamin - Nicolas J. S. Davies, "Hey, Hey, USA! How Many Bombs Did You Drop Today?" *Counterpunch*, January 13, 2022, https://www.counterpunch.org/2022/01/13/hey-hey-usa-how-many-bombs-did-you-drop-today.

25   Gareth Porter, "How McChrystal and Petraeus Built an Indiscriminate 'Killing Machine,'" *Truthout*, September 26, 2011, https://truthout.org/articles/how-mcchrystal-and-petraeus-built-an-indiscriminate-killing-machine.

26 "Iraq Coalition Casualty Count," http://icasualties.org (accessed April 12, 2024).

27 "Full text of the joint declaration," *The Guardian*, March 5, 2003, https://www.theguardian.com/world/2003/mar/06/france.germany.

28 Congressional Research Service, "Post-War Iraq: Foreign Contributions to Training,

Peacekeeping, and Reconstruction," Federation of American Scientists, September 25, 2007, https://sgp.fas.org/crs/mideast/RL32105.pdf.

29 Tracy Wilkinson, "Italians Honor 19 'Dear Heroes' Killed in Iraqi Truck Bombing," *Los Angeles Times*, November 19, 2003, https://www.latimes.com/archives/la-xpm-2003-nov-19-fg-italy19-story.html.

30 Patrice Claude, "The CIA's main man in Baghdad," *The Guardian*, July 23, 2004, https://www.theguardian.com/theguardian/2004/jul/23/guardianweekly.guardianweekly1.

31 UN Assistance Mission for Iraq (UNAMI), "Human Rights Report 1 July -3 August 2006," Global Security, https://www.globalsecurity.org/military///library/report/2006/hr-report_unami_jul-aug2006.htm (accessed April 12, 2024).

32 Congressional Research Service, "Post-War Iraq."

33 Medea Benjamin - Nicolas J. S. Davies, "Hey, Hey, USA!"

34 Gareth Porter, "How America Armed Terrorists in Syria," *The American Conservative*, June 22, 2017, https://www.theamericanconservative.com/how-america-armed-terrorists-in-syria.

35 "Iraq Coalition Casualty Count."

36 Garikai Chengu, "Gaddafi's Libya was Africa's Most Prosperous Democracy," *Foreign Policy Journal*, January 12, 2013, https://www.foreignpolicyjournal.com/2013/01/12/gaddafis-libya-was-africas-most-prosperous-democracy.

37 Mary Lynn Cramer, "Before US-NATO Invasion, Libya Had The Highest Human Development Index, The Lowest Infant Mortality, The Highest Life Expectancy In All Of Africa," *Counter Currents*, May 4, 2011, https://www.countercurrents.org/cramer040511.htm.

38 C.Y. Kwanue, "Liberia Hands Over US$65M Projects to Libya: Bong Co to Benefit," Iberian Observer via Bong County Association Of Georgia, January 25, 2011, https://bcagnews.wordpress.com/2011/01/25/liberia-hands-over-us65m-projects-to-libya-bong-co-to-benefit.

39 Amandla Thomas-Johnson and Simon Hooper, "'Sorted' by MI5: How UK government sent British-Libyans to fight Gaddafi," *Middle East Eye*, November 7, 2018, https://www.middleeasteye.net/news/sorted-mi5-how-uk-government-sent-british-libyans-fight-gaddafi.

40 United Nations Security Council, "Security Council Approves 'No-Fly Zone' over Libya, Authorizing 'All Necessary Measures' to Protect Civilians, by Vote of 10 in Favour with 5 Abstentions," United Nations, March 17, 2011, https://press.un.org/en/2011/sc10200.doc.htm#Resolution.

41 Alex DeWaal, "The African Union and the Libya Conflict of 2011," World Peace Foundation, December 19, 2012, https://sites.tufts.edu/reinventingpeace/2012/12/19/the-african-union-and-the-libya-conflict-of-2011.

42   C. J. Chivers and Eric Schmitt, "In Strikes on Libya by NATO, an Unspoken Civilian Toll," *The New York Times*, December 17, 2011, https://www.nytimes.com/2011/12/18/world/africa/scores-of-unintended-casualties-in-nato-war-in-libya.html.

43   BNO News, "Report: More than 250 Gaddafi supporters found dead in Sirte," Channel 6 via WayBackMachine, October 26, 2011, https://web.archive.org/web/20111028205828/http://channel6newsonline.com/2011/10/report-more-than-250-gaddafi-supporters-found-dead-in-sirte.

44   Patrick Wintour and Jessica Elgot, "MPs deliver damning verdict on David Cameron's Libya intervention," *The Guardian*, September 14, 2016, https://www.theguardian.com/world/2016/sep/14/mps-deliver-damning-verdict-on-camerons-libya-intervention.

45   Human Rights Watch, "Libya: Stop Arbitrary Arrests of Black Africans," Human Rights Watch, September 4, 2011, https://www.hrw.org/news/2011/09/04/libya-stop-arbitrary-arrests-black-africans.

46   U.S. Department of State, "U.S. Foreign Assistance By Country," foreignassistance.gov, https://www.foreignassistance.gov/cd/libya/2023/obligations/1 (accessed April 12, 2024).

4: NATO in Ukraine, But No Ukraine in NATO?

1   NATO, "Ukrainian PfP Training Centre," NATO.int, https://www.nato.int/structur/nmlo/links/yavoriv-training-centre.pdf (accessed April 12, 2024).

2   Wikipedia, "Ukrainian involvement in the Iraq War,"
     Wikipedia, https://en.wikipedia.org/wiki/Ukrainian_
     involvement_in_the_Iraq_War (accessed April 12, 2024).

3   William J. Burns, *The Back Channel: A Memoir of American
     Diplomacy and the Case for Its Renewal*. New York:
     Random House, 2020.

4   William J. Burns, "Nyet Means Nyet: Russia's NATO
     Enlargement Redlines," WikiLeaks, February 1, 2008,
     https://wikileaks.org/plusd/cables/08MOSCOW265_a.
     html.

5   Razumkof Centre, "Ukraine Poll," WayBackMachine,
     https://web.archive.org/web/20140502193915/http://www.
     razumkov.org.ua/eng/poll.php?poll_id=46 (accessed April
     12, 2024).

6   NATO, "Vilnius Summit Communiqué," NATO.int, July
     11, 2023, https://www.nato.int/cps/en/natohq/official_
     texts_217320.htm.

7   "Ukraine crisis: 300 US paratroopers arrive in western
     Ukraine to train national guard, US army says," ABC, April
     17, 2015, https://www.abc.net.au/news/2015-04-17/300-us-
     troops-arrive-in-ukraine-to-train-local-military/6402124.

8   "Joint Multinational Training Group-Ukraine," 7th Army
     Training Command, https://www.7atc.army.mil/JMTGU.

9   The New Voice of Ukraine, "German MP says Merkel
     shares responsibility for war in Ukraine as ex-chancellor
     blocked Ukraine from NATO," Yahoo, March 3, 2023,
     https://news.yahoo.com/german-mp-says-merkel-
     shares-142500321.html?guccounter=1.

10   Lucian Kim, "How U.S. Military Aid Has Helped Ukraine Since 2014," NPR, December 18, 2019, https://www.npr.org/2019/12/18/788874844/how-u-s-military-aid-has-helped-ukraine-since-2014.

11   Modern Diplomacy, "Merkel's confession could be a pretext for an International Tribunal," *Modern Diplomacy*, December 13, 2022, https://moderndiplomacy.eu/2022/12/13/merkels-confession-could-be-a-pretext-for-an-international-tribunal.

12   "IntelBrief: The Transnational Network That Nobody is Talking About," The Soufan Center, March 22, 2019, https://thesoufancenter.org/intelbrief-the-transnational-network-that-nobody-is-talking-about.

13   Guy Faulconbridge and Darya Korsunskaya, "Putin's suggestion of Ukraine ceasefire rejected by United States, sources say," Reuters, February 13, 2024, https://www.reuters.com/world/europe/putins-suggestion-ukraine-ceasefire-rejected-by-united-states-sources-say-2024-02-13.

14   James Keaton, "NATO chief fears Ukraine war could become a wider conflict," Associated Press, December 9, 2022, https://apnews.com/article/russia-ukraine-jens-stoltenberg-government-f01121d326938819920b1fe5e8c75b22d.

15   Brett Samuels, "Biden: Direct conflict between NATO and Russia would be 'World War III'," *The Hill*, March 11, 2022, https://thehill.com/policy/international/597842-biden-direct-conflict-between-nato-and-russia-would-be-world-war-iii.

5: NATO "Partners" Around the Globe

1   NATO, "Tripartite Draft Reply to Soviet Note of March
    31," NATO.int, April 24, 1954, https://archives.nato.int/
    uploads/r/null/3/7/37267/RDC_54_215_BIL.pdf.

2   Sergey Radchenko, Timothy Andrews Sayle, Christian
    F. Ostermann, eds., *NATO in the Cold War and After:
    Contested Histories and Future Directions*. London and
    New York: Routledge, 2022.

3   Jennifer Rankin, "Ex-Nato head says Putin wanted to join
    alliance early on in his rule," *The Guardian*, November 4,
    2021, https://www.theguardian.com/world/2021/nov/04/
    ex-nato-head-says-putin-wanted-to-join-alliance-early-
    on-in-his-rule.

4   Mark Perry, "The U.S. Army's War Over Russia," *Politico*,
    May 12, 2016, https://www.politico.com/magazine/
    story/2016/05/army-internal-fight-russia-defense-
    budget-213885.

5   Freedom House, "Countries and Territories," Freedom
    House, https://freedomhouse.org/countries/freedom-
    world/scores?sort=asc&order=Total%20Score%20
    and%20Status (accessed April 12, 2024).

6   "2022 Country Reports on Human Rights Practices," US
    Department of State, March 20, 2023, https://www.state.gov/
    reports/2022-country-reports-on-human-rights-practices/.

7   "Philippines, U.S. & NATO Military Prepare for
    Deployments to Batanes Near Taiwan," US Military
    District, February 17, 2024, https://www.youtube.com/
    watch?v=ObfZCITVIaM.

8   "Partnership interoperability initiative," NATO, March 7, 2024, https://www.nato.int/cps/en/natohq/topics_132726.htm.

9   "NATO 2020: United for a New Era," NATO, November 25, 2020, https://www.nato.int/nato_static_fl2014/assets/pdf/2020/12/pdf/201201-Reflection-Group-Final-Report-Uni.pdf.

10   "NATO 2030: A more united and stronger alliance on the global stage," NATO, https://www.nato-pa.int/download-file?filename=/sites/default/files/2020-12/2020%20-%20NATO%20PA%20DECLARATION%20460.pdf.

11   "SIPRI Arms Transfers Database," SIPRI, https://www.sipri.org/databases/armstransfers.

12   John T Psaropoulos, "Fear of China, Russia and Iran is driving weapons sales," Al Jazeera, March 11, 2024, https://www.aljazeera.com/news/2024/3/11/fear-of-china-russia-and-iran-is-driving-weapons-sales-report#:~:text=US%20remains%20the%20biggest%20arms,34%20percent%20in%202013%2D18.

13   Pavel Polityuk, "Japan minister, in Kyiv bomb shelter, pledges funds to fight drones," Reuters, January 7, 2024, https://www.reuters.com/world/japans-foreign-minister-visits-ukraine-2024-01-07/

14   "Dialogues focus on NATO-Private Sector 2030 initiative, NATO, June 2, 2021, https://www.nato.int/cps/en/natohq/news_184601.htm.

15   "SIPRI Military Expenditure Database," SIPRI, https://www.sipri.org/databases/milex.

16   "NATO Military Committee receives brief on Israeli
      approach to military innovation," NATO, May 8, 2023,
      https://www.nato.int/cps/en/natohq/news_214458.
      htm?selectedLocale=en

17   https://www.972mag.com/lavender-ai-israeli-army-gaza/.

18   Yuval Abraham, "'Lavender': The AI machine directing Israel's
      bombing spree in Gaza," *+972 Magazine*, April 3, 2024, https://
      www.cnn.com/middleeast/live-news/israel-news-hamas-
      war-10-12-23/h_4394d301cfff37d048a0f1a531a26e68.

19   "Europe slow to join US-led Red Sea mission against
      Huthis," France24, January 16, 2024, https://www.france24.
      com/en/live-news/20240116-europe-slow-to-join-us-led-
      red-sea-mission-against-huthis.

20   Dan Sabbagh, "US announces naval coalition to defend
      Red Sea shipping from Houthi attacks," *The Guardian*,
      December 19, 2023, https://www.theguardian.com/
      us-news/2023/dec/19/us-announces-naval-coalition-to-
      defend-red-sea-shipping-from-houthi-attacks.

21   Andrew Grey, "EU's Borrell suggests US cut military aid
      to Israel," Reuters, February 12, 2024, https://www.reuters.
      com/world/eus-borrell-suggests-us-rethink-military-aid-
      israel-2024-02-12/.

22   https://twitter.com/MartinKonecny/status/
      1752715347449274802.

23   Kate Abnett, "EU diplomat says defunding U.N.
      Palestinian agency would be dangerous," February 4,
      2024, *The Guardian*, https://www.reuters.com/world/
      middle-east/eu-diplomat-says-defunding-un-palestinian-
      agency-would-be-dangerous-2024-02-04/.

6: Who Makes the Decisions and Who Pays?

1   "The Secretary General's Annual Report: 2023," NATO, https://www.nato.int/nato_static_fl2014/assets/pdf/2024/3/pdf/sgar23-en.pdf.

2   "Case against Tommy Franks Dismissed," Al Jazeera, September 23, 2003, https://www.aljazeera.com/news/2003/9/23/case-against-tommy-franks-dismissed.

3   Ian Black, "US threatens Nato boycott over Belgian war crimes law," The Guardian, June 13, 2003, https://www.theguardian.com/world/2003/jun/13/nato.warcrimes.

4   "Romanian President Iohannis to run for NATO leadership," Reuters, March 12, 2024, https://www.reuters.com/world/europe/romanian-president-says-he-will-run-nato-leadership-2024-03-12/.

5   Lucy Sarret, "NATO's largest European military base begins construction in Romania," MSN Daily Express, https://www.msn.com/en-us/news/world/natos-largest-european-military-base-begins-construction-in-romania/ar-BB1k6j18.

6   James FitzGerald, "Trump says he would 'encourage' Russia to attack Nato allies who do not pay their bills," February 11, 2024, https://www.bbc.com/news/world-us-canada-68266447.

7   Michael Gold, "Trump Says He Gave NATO Allies Warning: Pay In or He'd Urge Russian Aggression," *The New York Times*, February 10, 2024, https://www.nytimes.com/2024/02/10/us/politics/trump-nato-russia.html.

8   "Funding NATO," NATO, April 5, 2024, https://www.nato.
     int/cps/en/natohq/topics_67655.htm.

9   Robert Pollin and Heidi Garrett-Peltier,"The U.S.
     Employment Effects of Military and Domestic
     Spending Priorities: 2011 Update," Political Economy
     Research Institute, https://scholarworks.umass.edu/
     cgi/viewcontent.cgi?article=1122&context=peri_
     workingpapers

10   https://twitter.com/davidcnswanson/
     status/1757026778533564511.

11   World BEYOND War, "We Need $2 Trillion/Year for Other
     Things," World BEYOND War https://worldbeyondwar.
     org/2trillion (accessed April 14, 2024).

7: How Does NATO Relate to the UN and International Law?

1   James Dobbins et al, "Overextending and Unbalancing
     Russia," RAND, April 24, 2019, https://www.rand.org/pubs/
     research_briefs/RB10014.html.

2   NIAC, "Organizations Tell U.S. Congress to Tell Us What
     Sanctions Do," World BEYOND War, August 5, 2022,
     https://worldbeyondwar.org/organizations-tell-u-s-
     congress-to-tell-us-what-sanctions-do/.

3   "Strikes by US and Britain against Houthi forces were
     defensive," Reuters, January 12, 2024, https://www.reuters.
     com/world/middle-east/strikes-by-us-britain-against-
     houthi-forces-were-defensive-nato-2024-01-12/.

4   Denitsa Koseva, "Bosnian president appeals to US and
    Nato to prevent new war NBE Intellinews," January 11,
    2024. https://www.intellinews.com/bosnian-president-
    appeals-to-us-and-nato-to-prevent-new-war-307372.

5   Secretary General Jens Stoltenberg, Opening Remarks,
    NATO, September 7, 2023, https://www.nato.int/cps/en/
    natohq/opinions_218172.htm?selectedLocale=en.

8: NATO and Nuclear Weapons

1   NATO Nuclear Deterrence, NATO, February 2020. https://
    www.nato.int/nato_static_fl2014/assets/pdf/2020/2/
    pdf/200224-factsheet-nuclear-en.pdf.

2   Ludo De Brabander and Soetkin Van Muylem,
    NATO Practices Deployment of Nuclear Weapons in
    Belgium," World Beyond War, October 14, 2022. https://
    worldbeyondwar.org/nato-practices-deployment-of-
    nuclear-weapons-in-belgium/.

3   Hans Kristensen et al, "Status of World Nuclear Forces,"
    Federation of American Scientists, March 31, 2023, https://
    fas.org/issues/nuclear-weapons/status-world-nuclear-
    forces/.

4   Matt Precey, "Are US nuclear weapons set to return to
    RAF Lakenheath?," BBC, February 18, 2024, https://www.
    bbc.com/news/uk-england-suffolk-68217519.

5   Nuclear Disarmament NATO, Nuclear Threat Initiative,
    January 17, 2024, https://www.nti.org/analysis/articles/
    nato-nuclear-disarmament/.

6   Scott Neuman, "U.S. 'Show Of Force' After Turkish-Backed Fighters Get Too Close To Base In Syria," NPR, October 15, 2019, https://www.npr.org/2019/10/15/770209247/u-s-imposes-sanctions-on-turkey-for-invasion-of-syria.

7   Michael S. Schmidt, "'There's Something Going On in Turkey,' U.S. Colonel Was Told During Coup Attempt," *The New York Times*, August 2, 2016, https://www.nytimes.com/2016/08/03/world/europe/turkey-coup-incirlik-air-base.html.

8   "Fact Sheet: US Nuclear Weapons in Europe, Center for Arms Control and Non-Proliferation," August 18, 2021, https://armscontrolcenter.org/fact-sheet-u-s-nuclear-weapons-in-europe/.

9   "Remarks by President Barack Obama in Prague," The White House, April 5, 2009, https://obamawhitehouse.archives.gov/the-press-office/remarks-president-barack-obama-prague-delivered.

10 Ambassador Jack Matlock, "America Relies on War for Jobs?," YouTube, July 29, 2016, https://www.youtube.com/watch?v=VdypP11X2P8.

11 Julian Borger, "US nuclear weapons: first low-yield warheads roll off the production line," *The Guardian*, January 28, 2019, https://www.theguardian.com/world/2019/jan/28/us-nuclear-weapons-first-low-yield-warheads-roll-off-the-production-line.

12 Dan Zak, "Meet the nuke the U.S. keeps in Europe, waiting to not be used," *The Washington Post*, March 25, 2022, https://www.washingtonpost.com/lifestyle/2022/03/25/nuclear-weapon-b61-russia/.

13 Sebastien Robbin, "The F-35 Is Now the World's
    First Stealth Fighter Certified to Carry a Nuke,"
    Popular Mechanics, March 8, 2024, https://www.
    popularmechanics.com/military/aviation/a60141719/f35-
    certified-to-carry-a-nuke/.

14 Edmond Seay, "NATO's Incredible Nuclear Strategy: Why
    U.S. Weapons in Europe Deter No One," Arms Control
    Association, https://www.armscontrol.org/act/2011-11/
    natos-incredible-nuclear-strategy-why-us-weapons-
    europe-deter-one.

15 Dan Zak, "Meet the nuke the U.S. keeps in Europe, waiting
    to not be used," *The Washington Post*, March 25, 2022,
    https://www.washingtonpost.com/lifestyle/2022/03/25/
    nuclear-weapon-b61-russia/.

16 Jonathan Masters and Will Merrow, "Nuclear Weapons in
    Europe: Mapping U.S. and Russian Deployments," Council
    on Foreign Relations, March 30, 2023, https://www.cfr.
    org/in-brief/nuclear-weapons-europe-mapping-us-and-
    russian-deployments.

17 Buchel Action, "Peace Activists Gain Entry to German Air
    Base that Holds US Nuclear Bombs," World BEYOND War,
    July 15, 2018, https://worldbeyondwar.org/peace-activists-
    gain-entry-to-german-air-base-that-holds-us-nuclear-
    bombs/.

18 Brendon Boyle, "Holland holds biggest anti-war
    protest," UPI, November 21, 1981, https://www.upi.com/
    Archives/1981/11/21/Holland-holds-biggest-anti-war-
    protest/3152375166800/.

19 Alexandra Brzozowski, "Belgium Debates Phase-Out Of US Nuclear Weapons On Its Soil," World BEYOND War, January 21, 2019, https://worldbeyondwar.org/belgium-debates-phase-out-of-us-nuclear-weapons-on-its-soil/.

20 Nina Werkhäuser, "US set to upgrade its nukes in Germany," DW, March 26, 2020, https://www.dw.com/en/us-set-to-upgrade-controversial-nukes-stationed-in-germany/a-52855886

21 Alice Slater, "On the 50th Anniversary of the Non-Proliferation Treaty: An Exercise in Bad Faith," World BEYOND War, June 30, 2018. https://worldbeyondwar.org/on-the-50th-anniversary-of-the-non-proliferation-treaty-an-exercise-in-bad-faith/.

9: What Are the Divisions Within NATO?

1 "NATO 2030: United for a New Era," NATO, November 25, 2020, https://www.nato.int/nato_static_fl2014/assets/pdf/2020/12/pdf/201201-Reflection-Group-Final-Report-Uni.pdf.

2 Jordan Cohen, "Turkey is a US ally, but should not be a trusted one," *The Hill*, December 31, 2023, https://thehill.com/opinion/4383282-turkey-is-a-us-ally-but-should-not-be-a-trusted-one/.

3 Miranda Bryant, "Sweden's Kurds fear Nato deal has sold them out," *The Guardian*, February 7, 2024, https://www.theguardian.com/world/2024/feb/07/now-we-are-not-safe-swedens-kurds-fear-nato-deal-has-sold-them-out.

4   Richard Boudreaux and Amberin Zaman, "Turkey Rejects U.S. Troop Deployment," *Los Angeles Times*, March 2, 2003, https://www.latimes.com/archives/la-xpm-2003-mar-02-fg-iraq2-story.html.

5   Marton Kasnyik, "Hungary to Allow Sweden Into NATO Following Jet Fighter Deal," Bloomberg, February 23, 2024, https://www.bloomberg.com/news/articles/2024-02-23/hungary-s-orban-to-agree-arms-deal-with-sweden-before-nato-vote.

6   Andreas Rinke and Guy Faulconbridge, "NATO allies rule out sending troops to Ukraine as Russia rebukes Macron,", February 27, 2024, https://www.reuters.com/world/europe/europeans-rule-out-sending-troops-ukraine-russia-rebukes-macron-2024-02-27/.

7   Maegan Vazquez, "Congress approves bill barring presidents from unilaterally exiting NATO," December 18, 2023, https://www.washingtonpost.com/national-security/2023/12/16/congress-nato-exit-trump/.

10: What Are the Divisions Within NATO?

1   "NATO 2030: A More United and Stronger Alliance on the Global Stage," Declaration 460, NATO Parliamentary Assembly, https://www.nato-pa.int/download-file?filename=/sites/default/files/2020-12/2020%20-%20NATO%20PA%20DECLARATION%20460.pdf.

2   James Dobbins et al, "Overextending and Unbalancing Russia," RAND Research Brief, April 24,

2019, https://www.rand.org/pubs/research_briefs/
RB10014.html.

3   Nicolas Camut, "Putin could attack NATO in '5 to 8 years,'
German defense minister warns," *Politico*, January 19,
2024, https://www.politico.eu/article/vladimir-putin-
russia-germany-boris-pistorius-nato/.

4   "Danish defence minister warns Russia could attack
NATO in 3-5 years," Reuters, February 9, 2024, https://
www.reuters.com/world/europe/danish-defence-
minister-warns-russia-could-attack-nato-3-5-years-
media-2024-02-09/.

5   Nicolas Camut, "Putin could attack NATO in '5 to 8 years,'
German defense minister warns," *Politico*, January 19,
2024, https://www.politico.eu/article/vladimir-putin-
russia-germany-boris-pistorius-nato/.

6   Sylvie Corbet, "Putting Western troops on the ground
in Ukraine is not 'ruled out' in the future," AP News,
February 26, 2024, https://apnews.com/article/paris-
conference-support-ukraine-zelenskyy-c458a1df3f9a76261
28cdeb84050d469.

7   Kaitlin Lewis, "NATO Moving Missiles Closer To Russia's
Borders," *Newsweek*, March 9, 2024, https://www.
newsweek.com/nato-moving-missiles-closer-russias-
borders-1877490.

8   Isabel van Brugen, "Are American Troops Fighting
in Ukraine," *Newsweek*, April 14, 2023,
https://www.newsweek.com/us-intelligence-pentagon-
leaks-american-us-troops-ukraine-jack-teixeira-
1794405

9   Julian Barnes, "Critical moment behind Ukraine's rapid advance in the east and south," *The New York Times*, September 14, 2022, https://buffalonews.com/critical-moment-behind-ukraines-rapid-advance-in-the-east-and-south/article_8d35f6d3-4bb0-54c9-8959-2ef46e7c21lf.html.

10   Isabelle Khurshudyan, "Ukraine's rocket campaign reliant on U.S. precision targeting," The Washington Post, February 9, 2023, https://archive.is/csVol.

11   "Agreement on Security co-operation between the United Kingdom of Great Britain and Northern Ireland and Ukraine," UK Government Publishing Service, January 12, 2024, https://assets.publishing.service.gov.uk/media/65a14a6ae96df50014f845d2/UK-Ukraine_Agreement_on_Security_Co-operation.pdf.

12   "Estonia announces security agreement with Ukraine, European Pravda, https://www.msn.com/en-us/news/world/estonia-announces-security-agreement-with-ukraine/ar-BBljzyi8.

13   Tetiana Herasimova, "Ukraine and Greece begin preparing bilateral agreement on security guarantees," Ukranews.com, March 6, 2024, https://ukranews.com/en/news/989834-ukraine-and-greece-begin-preparing-bilateral-agreement-on-security-guarantees-zelenskyy.

14   Tom Balmforth and Yuliia Dysa, "What are the security deals Ukraine is signing with allies?," Reuters, April 3, 2024, https://www.reuters.com/world/europe/

what-are-security-deals-ukraine-is-discussing-with-allies-2024-02-23/.

15 David Brennan, "NATO Needs Russia 'Ruined' in Ukraine for Future Peace," *Newsweek*, December 29, 2023, https://www.newsweek.com/nato-needs-russia-ruined-ukraine-future-peace-1856390.

16 Natasha Bertrand, "Austin's assertion that US wants to 'weaken' Russia underlines Biden strategy shift," CNN, April 26, 2022, https://www.cnn.com/2022/04/25/politics/biden-administration-russia-strategy/index.html.

17 Rebecca Shabad, "Sen. Lindsey Graham defends calling for Russians to assassinate Putin," NBC News, March 4, 2022, https://www.nbcnews.com/politics/congress/sen-lindsey-graham-defends-calling-russians-assassinate-putin-rcna18703.

18 "NATO intercepted Russian military aircraft over 300 times in 2023," NATO, December 29, 2023, https://www.nato.int/cps/en/natohq/news_221598.htm?selectedLocale=en.

19 "NATO 2030: United for a New Era," NATO, November 25, 2020, page 26, https://www.nato.int/nato_static_fl2014/assets/pdf/2024/3/pdf/sgar23-en.pdf.

20 "NATO to hold biggest drills since Cold War with 90,000 troops," Reuters, January 18, 2024, https://www.reuters.com/world/europe/nato-kick-off-biggest-drills-decades-with-some-90000-troops-2024-01-18/.

21 Tamás Orbán, "Leaked German Defense Document Sketches out Russian War Scenario," The

European Conservative, January 15, 2024, https://europeanconservative.com/articles/news/leaked-german-defense-document-sketches-out-russian-war-scenario/.

22 Mark Pomerleau, "US, allies share skills and tactics at annual NATO cyber exercise," Defensescoop, January 9, 2024, https://defensescoop.com/2024/01/09/nato-cyber-coalition-exercise-share-skills-tactics/.

23 "Europe can't decide how to unplug from China," *The Economist*, May 15, 2023, https://www.economist.com/international/2023/05/15/europe-cant-decide-how-to-unplug-from-china.

24 "NATO 2030: United for a New Era," NATO, November 25, 2020, https://www.nato.int/nato_static_fl2014/assets/pdf/2020/12/pdf/201201-Reflection-Group-Final-Report-Uni.pdf.

25 "Secretary General appoints independent group as part of NATO reflection on southern neighbourhood," NATO, October 6, 2023, https://www.nato.int/cps/en/natohq/news_219076.htm?selectedLocale=en.

26 "NATO 2030: United for a New Era," NATO, November 25, 2020, https://www.nato.int/nato_static_fl2014/assets/pdf/2020/12/pdf/201201-Reflection-Group-Final-Report-Uni.pdf.

27 "NATO 2030: United for a New Era," NATO, November 25, 2020, https://www.nato.int/nato_static_fl2014/assets/pdf/2020/12/pdf/201201-Reflection-Group-Final-Report-Uni.pdf.

11: What Are the Alternatives?

1   "The Clock Shifts," Bulletin of the Atomic Scientists, https://thebulletin.org/doomsday-clock/timeline/.

2   Con Coughlin, "Putin is now openly planning for war against Nato," *The Telegraph*, March 21, 2024, https://www.telegraph.co.uk/news/2024/03/21/putin-now-openly-planning-for-war-against-nato/.

3   "Why End War," World BEYOND War, https://worldbeyondwar.org/why/.

4   David Swanson, "Growing List of Successful Nonviolent Actions Used Instead of Wars," World Beyond War, https://worldbeyondwar.org/list.

5   Meredith Bennett-Smith, "Womp! This Country Was Named The Greatest Threat To World Peace," *HuffPost*, January 2, 2014, https://www.huffpost.com/entry/greatest-threat-world-peace-country_n_4531824.

6   Dorothy Manevich, "Globally, more people see U.S. power and influence as a major threat," Pew Research Center, August 1, 2017, https://www.pewresearch.org/short-reads/2017/08/01/u-s-power-and-influence-increasingly-seen-as-threat-in-other-countries/.

7   Patrick Wintour, US seen as bigger threat to democracy than Russia or China," *The Guardian*, May 5, 2021, https://www.theguardian.com/world/2021/may/05/us-threat-democracy-russia-china-global-poll.

8   Laura Kelly, "Arab world holds overwhelmingly negative view of the US over support for Israel," *The Hill*, February 8, 2024, https://thehill.com/policy/

international/4456934-arab-world-poll-negative-view-
us-israel/.

9   Ethan Sager, "NATO's Leadership Faces Tougher Audience
    Outside Its Membership," Gallup, July 18, 2023, https://
    news.gallup.com/opinion/gallup/508766/nato-leadership-
    faces-tougher-audience-outside-membership.aspx.

10 Lorna Bogue, "No, Ireland Shouldn't Join NATO," *Jacobin*,
    October 4, 2023, https://jacobin.com/2023/10/ireland-
    nato-neutrality-forum-geopolitics-military.

11 "Record 83% of Ukrainians want NATO membership,"
    Reuters, October 3, 2022, https://www.reuters.com/world/
    europe/record-83-ukrainians-want-nato-membership-
    poll-2022-10-03/.

12 Ben Thompson, "Perspectives on NATO from the
    Outside," International Republican Institute, July 21, 2023,
    https://www.iri.org/news/perspectives-on-nato-from-the-
    outside/.

13 Moira Fagan, "Views of NATO," Pew Research
    Center, July 10, 2023, https://www.pewresearch.org/
    global/2023/07/10/views-of-nato/.

14 Mohamed Yunis, "Americans Remain Committed
    to NATO, Critical of UN," Gallup, February 29, 2024,
    https://news.gallup.com/poll/611261/americans-remain-
    committed-nato-critical.aspx.

15 "Save Sinjajevina," World BEYOND War, October 7, 2021,
    https://worldbeyondwar.org/sinjajevina/.

16 Nukewatch, "U.S. Peace Activist Given Prison Term in
    German Campaign to Oust U.S. Nuclear Bombs," World
    BEYOND War, March 11, 2024, https://worldbeyondwar.

org/u-s-peace-activist-given-prison-term-in-german-campaign-to-oust-u-s-nuclear-bombs/.

17   Vienna Collucci, "We Get It," Amnesty International, May 19, 2012, https://blog.amnestyusa.org/asia/we-get-it/.

18   "No to NATO, Yes to Peace," World BEYOND War, April 3, 2019, https://worldbeyondwar.org/notonato/.

About the Authors

MEDEA BENJAMIN is the co-founder of the women-led peace group CODEPINK. She is also co-founder of the human rights group Global Exchange, the Peace in Ukraine Coalition, Unfreeze Afghanistan (which advocates for returning the $7 billion of Afghan funds frozen in U.S. banks), and ACERE: The Alliance for Cuba Engagement and Respect.

Medea has been an advocate for social justice for 50 years. Described as "one of America's most committed—and most effective—fighters for human rights" by *New York Newsday*, and "one of the high profile leaders of the peace movement" by the *Los Angeles Times*, she was one of 1,000 exemplary women from 140 countries nominated to receive the Nobel Peace Prize on behalf of the millions of women who do the essential work of peace worldwide.

She is the author of ten books, including *Drone Warfare: Killing by Remote Control*, *Kingdom of the Unjust: Behind the U.S.-Saudi Connection*, *Inside Iran:*

The Real History and Politics of the Islamic Republic of Iran, and coauthor, with Nicolas J.S. Davies, of *War in Ukraine: Making Sense of a Senseless Conflict.* Her articles appear regularly in outlets such as *The Hill, Salon, CommonDreams* and *The Progressive.* You can find her frequent posts and videos on social media at @medeabenjamin.

DAVID SWANSON is an author, activist, journalist, and radio host. He is executive director of World BEYOND War and campaign coordinator for RootsAction.org. Swanson's books include *War Is A Lie* and *When the World Outlawed War.* He blogs at DavidSwanson.org and WarIsACrime.org. He hosts Talk World Radio. He is a Nobel Peace Prize Nominee.

Swanson was awarded the 2018 Peace Prize by the U.S. Peace Memorial Foundation. He was also awarded a Beacon of Peace Award by the Eisenhower Chapter of Veterans For Peace in 2011, and the Dorothy Eldridge Peacemaker Award by New Jersey Peace Action in 2022, and a Global Peace Leadership & Excellence Award in 2024.

Swanson is on the advisory boards of: Nobel Peace Prize Watch, Veterans For Peace, Assange Defense, BPUR, Military Families Speak Out, Fields of Peace, and Peace in Ukraine Coalition. He is an Associate of

180

the Transnational Foundation, and a Patron of Platform for Peace and Humanity. He is on the Consultative Council of the SHAPE Project. He is on the International Coordinating Committee of No to War – No to NATO.

Find Swanson on social media as @davidcnswanson.